THE PERIPATETIC SAYING

Number 89
THE PERIPATETIC SAYING
The Problem of the Thrice-Told Tale
in Talmudic Literature

by
Jacob Neusner

THE PERIPATETIC SAYING
The Problem of the Thrice-Told Tale
in Talmudic Literature

by
Jacob Neusner

Scholars Press
Chico, California

THE PERIPATETIC SAYING
The Problem of the Thrice-Told Tale in Talmudic Literature

by
Jacob Neusner

Library of Congress Cataloging in Publication Data

Neusner, Jacob, 1932–
   The peripatetic saying.

   (Brown Judaic studies ; no. 89)
   Includes index.
   1. Aggada—History and criticism. 2. Pharisees—Legends—
History and criticism. I. Title. II. Series: Brown Judaic studies ;
no. 89.
BM516.5.N48 1985   296.1'27606   84–27583
ISBN 0–89130–830–X (alk. paper)
ISBN 0–89130–831–8 (pbk. : alk. paper)

Printed in the United States of America
on acid-free paper

For

Tsvi Groner

A fine scholar and a good citizen of the world of
Jewish learning, who, under trying circumstances,
has made for himself a life and an important career
in the study of the formative age of Judaism, and who
continues to ornament the world in which he works.

CONTENTS

Preface   1

I
THE BAVLI AT THE END

I. The Bavli at the End. A Canonical Perspective on the Problem of the   7
   Peripatetic Saying

   i.   Introduction   7
   ii. From the Yerushalmi to the Fathers According to Rabbi Nathan
       to the Bavli   17
   iii. From the Sifre on Deuteronomy to the Bavli   21
   iv. From the Yerushalmi to the Bavli. Two Cases.   22
   v.   From Josephus to the Bavli   25
   vi. The Bavli at the End   29

II
THE THRICE-TOLD TALE IN RABBINIC STORIES
ABOUT PHARISEES BEFORE 70

II. Simeon the Just   33

III. Antigonos of Sokho. Yose b. Yoezer and Yose b. Yohanan   49

IV. Joshua b. Perahiah and Nittai the Arbelite. Judah b. Tabbai and
    Simeon b. Shetah   55

V. Shemaiah and Abtalion   79

VI. Yohanan the High Priest   85

VII. Menaham. Shammai   93

VIII. Hillel   97

CONTENTS (continued)

IX. Shammai and Hillel   117

X. Gamaliel   125

XI. Simeon b. Gamaliel   131

XII. Yohanan b. Zakkai   135

III

THREE THEORIES OF THE PERIPATETIC SAYING

XIII. "He Often Used to Say"   151

XIV. In Search of the "Original" "Tradition"   159

XV. Incremental History: "When he was a student... and when he grew up..." 171

IV

CONCLUSION

XVI. A Documentary-Historical Theory   179

Appendix: Autonomy, Connection, Continuity: The Three Dimensions of a
          Text of Formative Judaism   191

Index   197

PREFACE

This is the third and last part of a trilogy on three principal methodological problems in the analysis of the literature of the canon of Judaism that began with the Mishnah, ca. A.D. 200, and concluded with the Talmud of Babylonia ("Bavli"), ca. A.D. 600. The first of the three problems occupied In Search of Talmudic Biography. The Problem of the Attributed Saying (Chico, 1984: Scholars Press for Brown Judaic Studies), the second, From Mishnah to Scripture. The Problem of the Unattributed Saying (Chico, 1984: Scholars Press for Brown Judaic Studies), and the third, the present volume. In all three books I make use of completed research to point up main lines of inquiry into a methodological issue transcending the limits of that earlier research. In Search of Talmudic Biography rested on my Eliezer ben Hyrcanus: The Tradition and the Man (Leiden, 1973: E.J. Brill) I-II. From Mishnah to Scripture stood in the same relationship to my History of the Mishnaic Law of Purities (Leiden, 1974-1977: E.J. Brill), I-XX. This book absorbs and revises parts of my Development of a Legend. Studies on the Traditions Concerning Yohanan ben Zakkai (Leiden, 1970: E.J. Brill), a chapter of Judaism in Conclusion. The Evidence of the Bavli (planned for publication later on), and, mainly, completed synoptic exercises of my Rabbinic Traditions about the Pharisees before 70 (Leiden, 1971) I. The Masters. As will be clear, the tables of comparisons of versions of stories given in that book form the shank of the present work. Here I amplify and vastly extend the discussion of the problem at hand in the chapter of Judaism in Conclusion devoted to the relationship of the Bavli's to the Yerushalmi's versions of the same materials.

In this way I wish to make available some of the results of inquiries originally conducted for quite separate purposes. After fifteen years, I realize that those earlier inquiries, devoted as much to methodological as to substantive problems, made their appropriate contribution principally to the substantive discussion of their topics. The larger methodological implications of the exercises demanded articulation and explanation I failed to supply. In restating the results in the present context of the trilogy at hand, I aim to correct that error in the presentation of my results. In this way I hope to call attention to the methodological implications of facts uncovered long ago and in a distant setting.

For the issue remains present and vivid: what, really, can we know about the formation of Judaism in late antiquity from the canon of Judaism of that age? How, actually, do we know it? To state the matter simply, I wish to explain what we are to do with attributions of sayings and stories to particular sages. I propose to show how we may deal with unattributed sayings and uncredited stories. Here I begin the work of sorting out which lessons we learn, and which reject, from the fact that the compilers of

successive documents include, in diverse versions, the same saying and the same story.
The guidelines of future research flow from the answers, based on facts, we find to these
problems in the limited exercises already accomplished. Here at last we confront the
bedrock questions of the formation not of the documents alone, but of large segments of
the prior compositions drawn together and included in those documents. So we move
deeper than we have been before into the formation of the raw materials of the system --
if not to the depths of the matter.

The idea for this book came to me as I worked on Chapter Eight of Judaism in
Conclusion: The Evidence of the Bavli. I realized that the issue of that chapter --
Yerushalmi-Bavli relationships -- required systematic treatment in a much broader setting
than defined there. I debated with myself whether or not to present, once more, a sizable
array of facts already in hand. I persuaded myself to take time out for such a project.
First, the passage of a decade and a half in which the facts at hand had attracted no
attention and made no contribution seemed to me to justify restating them, but with
appropriate emphasis. Second, my original failure to spell out precisely the implications I
saw in these facts seemed to me the principal error demanding correction. So in restating
the matter, I mean to spell out more clearly both my theory of what things mean and the
facts upon which any theory will have to rest.

So far as the primitives and the Israeli Talmudists continue to do historical work
(and they have given us remarkably little in a decade and a half), we shall continue to hear
about "once..., and then again..., and on yet a third occasion...." Works on the history of
the law, on the one side, and on the history of the "mystical tradition" (that is, the
chariot-vision and similar matters), on the other, have shamelessly assumed the incremental-historical theory of the literature which I explain in the introduction and illustrate
in Chapter Fifteen. The premises of that theory are expressed as best I can and measured
against data.

These facts, as I here amply demonstrate, point to a continuous literary history. It
is a history of people making changes, ordinarily additions, to stories and revisions, some
major, some minor, to sayings. This they did for reasons we do not know, in settings we
cannot identify, and for a larger purpose, program, and system, we cannot specify. To
impute reasons made up for the occasion, to claim to specify settings and context, to
allege we know what they were thinking and why -- these theses demand sustained
argument, analysis, even evidence. Exercises of verification and falsification cannot be
made up ad hoc for the occasion, item by item, merely as the author's larger purpose
demands. They have to confront the whole in its entirety.

I insist we see the literature as a canon, the stories as they flow, not hither and yon
but from document to document. What this means I explain in the appendix. Hence all
facts to begin with demand interpretation in the context of specific documents and their
larger traits. That is a sizable program, and, in my view, until it has yielded viable
generalizations of an encompassing character, all work resting on the incremental-historical method will have to await its appropriate hearing. For I see no point to argue
about details when the main premises demand rigorous definition, analysis, and demon-

stration. To make matters specific, if we do not know what a given document ordinarily does with a received saying or story, for instance, what the authors of the Yerushalmi are likely in general to wish to do to any saying or story they receive from the Tosefta or from Sifra or one of the Sifres, then we also do not know how to evaluate what they have done with a specific received saying or story.

Clearly, in moving so far as the present phrasing of matters, I have gone some distance from the discourse with the primitives and Israeli Talmudic historians. But no one who does not say what they want to hear can enter into discourse with them. They tell us that they will not listen, so we need not try any more. In any event the issue before us does not interest them. Why not? The primitives already "know" that whatever a story says really happened, and whatever people impute to a given sage really was said by him. So on the basis of perfect faith we can do history straight out, without the intervention of the considerations so troubling to this world of doubters and disbelievers. So be it. We shall do our work and watch them try to do theirs.

Readers who follow the current polemical literature will have wondered where and how I propose to reply to three remarkable discussions, in the tradition of Solomon Zeitlin, of books of mine.

Where, as in Journal of the American Oriental Society 104, 2, 1984, a critic supplies valued corrections of mistakes, I ignore the violent language and take over the criticisms as rapidly as possible. Saul Lieberman's diverse observations concerning my Talmud of the Land of Israel. A Preliminary Translation and Explanation. 33. Abodah Zarah have been worked into a list of corrections to be made, and printed in Talmud of the Land of Israel. A Preliminary Translation and Explanation. 23. Nedarim (Chicago, 1985: University of Chicago Press). When we ignore, as all scholars must, the obiter dicta Lieberman left as the testament of his character, we come up with about a page and a half of minor corrigenda. But all of them are valuable, though none of them makes much material difference to the main point of even the handful of paragraphs in which they occur. Would that we had a better text, dictionary, and commentary on which to base a preliminary translation. What Lieberman really reviewed and found wanting was his generation's accomplishments in Yerushalmi-studies. Had he provided the dictionary, the text, and the commentary, he would have found no reason to complain about my translation.

Where, as in Midstream, May 1984, an amateur, a learned journalist, has his say, and, as it happens, his say turns out to concern not the issues of method and substance that occupy true scholars, but contemporary theological and publicistic concerns, there is nothing to be learned, therefore nothing to be said in reply.

Where, as in Conservative Judaism, Vol. 37, 1, 1983 (which appeared in November, 1984), a rank beginner decides to turn scholarship into a blood sport, there is nothing to be said. Scholarly issues really are interesting when they can be discussed with mutual dignity and respect. But where the issues are framed, as in the Conservative-Judaic theological setting, in brutal and vile language, no serious interchange of ideas is possible. It is a pity. There really are issues worth pursuing.

Saul Lieberman, whatever else he was, was a scholar, who accomplished a considerable labor of talmudic exegesis. My other critics have nothing to teach the world. I accept this abuse in a spirit of humility and cheerfully confront slander and libel, because it is in the cause of the learning . I am glad that the defamation carried on in an other-than-public form for twenty-five years has now come to the public forum. The time has now arrived in which the nature of criticism and of the critics is there for all to see and assess. So we can get on with the task at hand. No one any longer needs to pay attention to ad hominem comments that prove, in the full light of day, to be deranged, or ignorant, or stupid, or merely silly. If truth be told, no scholar with a serious program of inquiry ever did pay much attention to political and theological side-shows. The main event remains what it always was, the description, analysis, and interpretation of the formative age of Judaism. When the critics have something to say about that problem, they will have their hearing and appropriate answers. I envy Rudolph Bultmann many things, but above all, I envy him Karl Barth. He had a critic worth serious discourse, and so far in the circle of Judaic learning I have not. But I remain confident that the future will hold for me and for the issues I address that serious and sustained, rigorous criticism, that I believe appropriate to the issues at hand and to the methodological and substantive dimensions of the debate.

The scholarly world in any event knows how to assess political, ad hominem attacks. Scholars nearly everywhere respect those canons of civil discourse that permit free interchange of differing opinions. To engage in public in this labor of description, analysis, and interpretation, we all accept risks of libel and slander. To respond to discourse of such unilluminating character as has recently soured scholarly exchange serves no constructive purpose. It merely demeans the dignity of learning. Were any of us who are engaged in investigating the formative history of Judaism to invest energies in defense against slander and murderous personal attacks, the work would suffer, but nothing would be gained. The only appropriate response, in Judaism, is in this prayer: Limeqalelai nafshi tidom. Anyhow, the witless editors of the Journal of the American Oriental Society and Midstream and Conservative Judaism did manage to spell my name right.

I owe to my co-worker, William Scott Green, and to my students of the present, Howard Eilberg-Schwartz, and Paul Flesher, thanks for the encouragement to undertake this book and the opportunity to discuss problems in its contents and composition.

J.N.

Program in Judaic Studies
Brown University
Providence, Rhode Island 02912-1826 U.S.A.

Ereb Sukkot 5745
October 10, 1984

PART ONE

THE BAVLI AT THE END

CHAPTER ONE
THE BAVLI AT THE END
A CANONICAL PERSPECTIVE ON THE PROBLEM OF THE
PERIPATETIC SAYING

Introduction

This book completes my trilogy on literary and historical problems in the study of the canon of Judaism, that collection of books, beginning with the Mishnah and ending with the Babylonian Talmud, definitive of Judaism for all times. The trilogy encompasses a question of history and origin, in From Mishnah to Scripture. The Problem of the Unattributed Saying (Chico, 1984: Scholars Press for Brown Judaic Studies). In that exercise I took up the issue of how to sort out the historical meanings and values of those sayings in the corpus of the rabbinic canon not attributed to named authorities. The series also encounters the complementary issue. This is the problem of sayings bearing names and how such sayings are to serve for the study of the formative history and religion of the canon at hand. It is In Search of Talmudic Biography. The Problem of the Attributed Saying (with the same publication data). I there propose a thesis on how to assess the historical value of the claim that a given figure had made a statement or participated in an event.

The concluding study is the present one. We take up yet a third considerable trait of the literature at hand, the recurrent use, in document after document, with revision and alteration, of a single saying or story. What does it mean when a saying moves from one document in the canon to yet another in that same canon? And how are we to interpret shifts and changes in versions of a tale as it is told over and over again in its journeys from one piece of writing to the next? These are the two issues at hand. As usual in my work, I begin with an overview of the problem and my simple approach to a solution to it. Then I present a sizable corpus of facts. Third I review theories adduced to explain how we are to sort out and make use of those facts. Finally, I place into context the (rather humble) proposal I wish to make to deal with the same facts.

Let me now spell out what I see as the issues in the first two works and in the present one. Three principal problems in the analysis of that canon as a whole prove critical. For these problems emerge from traits of all of the canonical documents equally and uniformly. They therefore transcend the lines of division marked by the beginnings and endings of particular compositions, e.g., the Mishnah, the Tosefta, the Sifra, the Yerushalmi, the Bavli, the several collections of scriptural exegeses ("midrashim"), and the like. (The appendix states the importance of these lines of division and how I have interpreted their meaning.) Accordingly, the three problems at hand carry us deep into the formation of all of the canon's several components. When we address these issues of literary-redactional meaning we find ourselves moving into the pre-history, in the formative period, of materials that, later on, take up positions firmly set within public and accessible documentary settings in the finished canon.

First, all documents contain sayings given in the names of individual sages. The appearance of named authorities by itself raises a simple historical question: did the named sage really say what is imputed to him? Did he do what people said he did?

Second, all documents take shape around structures uniformly lacking in imputed authorship, on the one side, and include sayings without sages' names attached, on the other. While some canonical writings, for instance the Mishnah and the Tosefta, are said to have been "written" by specific figures, Judah the Patriarch and Hiyya in the present instance, none bears so much as a superscription parallel to those that, in the Gospels, lay claim to a particular named authority as author. More critical, the vast and encompassing corpus of sayings and stories not identified with particular authorities presents yet another simple historical question: to what time, place, and circumstance do the anonymous sayings and stories testify? How, if at all, are we to make use of anonymous sayings and stories in the reconstruction of the history and formation of the canon, hence of the Judaism for which it stands?

Finally, to the issue of this book, some sayings and stories pass from one document to the next. We shall see how they gain or lose weight as they make the journey. In part two of this book I give many scores of examples of what happens as a given saying or story makes the trip from, e.g., the Mishnah to the Tosefta to the Yerushalmi to the Bavli. In so doing, I make abundantly clear that at hand is a substantial problem, more complex than the relationship of books of the Bible that go over the same matters, for instance, Deuteronomy as against parts of Genesis through Numbers, or Chronicles as against Samuel and Kings. What do the changes indicate and what do they mean? In another age the problem of parallel versions of what we now think was a single event (or, more accurately, a single original tale) found an easy solution. If we have three versions, then we know about three events. Hence in the Gospels' scholarship comes the famous postulate that in addition to the Sermon on the Mount, Jesus preached a Sermon on the Plain. In the Hebrew Scriptures, the slightly diverse versions of the Ten Commandments kept gainfully employed long generations of preachers. The several versions of creation and of human and Israelite history supplied by J, E, P, and D challenged the wits of exegetes for many centuries. The theory of simultaneous enunciation of the Ten Commandments in Exodus and in Deuteronomy ("Keep" and "Remember" the Sabbath day being stated by a single voice at a single moment!) kept at bay inappropriate doubt for so long as people did not give way to doubt. But what began as a serious answer to a challenge to faith in the literal historicity of the biblical tale long ago had come to signify poetry and theology, no longer to write history.

In the rabbinical canon, by contrast, historians took several versions of a story to indicate one of three possibilities. Either the sage at hand went around saying the same thing a lot. Thus if the same saying occurs in four passages but in the same sage's name, that sage said it four times ("he often used to say"). If the same saying is placed into the

mouths of two different sages, then "X and Y agreed that...." Or several versions of a
saying or story demand integration and harmonization to supply the single reliable and
accurate account of what really happened. That is to say, when we can reduce the
versions to their "original" form, we not only account for the later revisions. More
important, we know pretty much accurately what had actually been said or done. Or (very
commonly nowadays) we account for the inclusion of each detail of a saying or story --
among a variety of diverse details -- by making up a theory on where and how, by whom
and for what purpose, a given detail "might" or "would" have been added. Let me spell out
this third approach to the problem of the thrice-told tale, because it is characteristic of
the last century of scholarship and stands as the foundation of much work even now.
When we have a long sequence of versions of a single matter, for instance (as we shall see
below) the vision of the chariot described by Ezekiel as that vision was interpreted by
Eleazar b. Azariah to Yohanan b. Zakkai, each successive shift and change in the version
appearing in the earliest document to contain it will demand, and receive, a manufactured
explanation.

The first of these three theories of the meaning and historical significance of the
peripatetic saying serves mainly among the yeshiva-primitives and the Israeli Talmudic
historians. It hardly demands serious scrutiny. It falls into the class of marvels and
wonders, along with "Keep" and "Remember" in a single act of speech. Theologians and
decisors of law harmonize, drawing on all sources to make one point. Others do not have
to do so and people interested in the formative history to which stories and sayings attest
had best not do so. Our work demands studied description, analysis, and interpretation --
and not a leap of faith.

The second is a datum, mostly among the same circles. It hardly contradicts the
first but depends on the same fundamentalism.

The third proves popular among the more critical and up-to-date historians of the
Jews in late antiquity and of the religion, Judaism, in that same period. It is, to say the
least, premature, because it rests on infirm foundations. How so? The assumption that
each detail testifies to a given historical event or moment, different from other details in
the same literary construct, assumes two things. First, the details -- it is postulated --
represent things that really happened. So the premise reveals that same literalist
fundamentalism that the allegedly modern historians reject. Second, it is assumed that
the text at hand was preserved from the beginning exactly as it was written. Any change
exhibited by a later version of a saying or story has, therefore, to find its explanation.
Changes do not just happen, they are made for reason. The people who make them do so
for reasons that the scholar can report (as we shall see, with no evidence whatsoever).
Nothing lacks "significance" of the present sort, and everything demands its explanation.
No explanation covers everything; each item demands an ad hoc interpretation of its own.
So the text is studded with histories, each supplied for its distinct occasion, none
proposing to harmonize with or relate to the last or the next. Accordingly, it is theorized,
people took a text and rewrote it as new things happened. They then handed it on to
others who did the same. This literary theory awaits any sort of sustained argumentation,

not to mention documentation. But it generates such scholarship as now flourishes on the problem at hand, alas.

In this book I propose to reenter the question at hand at a fundamental level. Specifically, I want to assemble and interpret a few facts about the thrice-told tale and the peripatetic saying. On the basis of these facts fresh approaches to the same long-standing problem will open before us.

Specifically, in this chapter, I point to the simple fact that when stories move from earlier documents to the Bavli, the final component of the canon, in that last appearance they take on a full and complete character that versions appearing in earlier documents lack. Whether the movement is over two or more documents, e.g., from the Yerushalmi to The Fathers according to Rabbi Nathan to Bavli, or from the Mekhilta to the Tosefta to the Yerushalmi to the Bavli, or from the penultimate Talmud to the last, that is, from the Yerushalmi to the Bavli, the pattern is the same. The Bavli's authors persistently add details to what has gone before. When we consider that fact, we realize exactly how we must proceed.

The way forward lies through the study of the literary characteristics and prefer- ences exhibited by the successive documents, viewed one by one, as they receive and revise sayings and stories. We may state, as a theory based on substantial evidence, that the authors of the Bavli exhibit a preference for completing tales by adding missing details. The hypothesis therefore presents itself that the authors, editors, and redactors of other documents along these same lines will exhibit equally persistent and definitive traits, characteristic of their treatment of a diversity of versions of sayings and stories as they fall into their hands. Precisely how to define these changes and what to make of them, first of all, demands collection and classification, by document, of types of shifts and changes in stories. Once we dismiss as simply unlikely the notion that, because a saying recurs, therefore the person to whom it is ascribed said the saying a lot, we begin this other and, I think, better-founded inquiry into the continuities and changes of the sayings as they wend their way from document to document. We assume only what the facts at hand dictate, which is that we have in fact one and the same saying. We then ask what comparison of what is like from document to document tells us about what is unlike among those same documents. Since the saying is our fixed point of reference, our variable must derive from recurrent traits of the diverse documents that receive and revise the saying.

I state the hypothesis in its simplest form in Chapter One, with sole reference to the Bavli. In Chapters Two through Twelve, I lay out a sequence of sayings and stories assigned to successive named authorities or told about them. My purpose is to show, with a large and substantial sample, exactly what changes occur in the peripatetic sayings and stories. I do so by a sequence of synoptic tables. Here I compare in parallel, vertical columns, the way in which stories occur in several documents. I compare in horizontal lines the details of a saying, given item by item down the left side. Sometimes what shifts is wording. Other times what changes is the inclusion or exclusion of a detail. After each synoptic exercise, I say in my own words what I think the table indicates. As often as I can, I explain why I think the authors have made the changes that we discern. These synoptic tables derive from my Rabbinic Traditions about the Pharisees before 70 (Leiden, 1971) I. The Masters, and from my Development of a Legend. Studies on the Traditions Concerning Yohanan ben Zakkai (Leiden, 1970). The cumulative effect of the synoptic studies, in my judgment, serves not to settle but only to underline the question at hand. It will not invalidate the hypothesis I propose in response to the question. Only detailed studies of documents one by one, then in comparison and contrast to one another, will yield a nuanced and well-grounded theory of the matter.

In part three I proceed to take up the three theories of the peripatetic saying outlined just now. I wish simply to show how and we each theory proves inadequate to the data at hand.

In the case of the theory that recurrence of a saying here and there means that the person to whom it is imputed said it a lot, I show that that theory is impossible in one striking and important case.

In connection with the theory of an "original" "tradition" (at which point I explain the quotation marks used in the title of the chapter), I demonstrate that, if we recover what clearly is an "original" "tradition" we do not gain a great deal. That is to say, once we know what wording lies behind a set of parallel and probably interdependent compositions, which present their variations on the same set of words, we scarcely know more than we did when we recognize that the several versions do vary the same set of words. So the quest for an "original" "tradition" yields trivialities.

In connection with the third theory of how to interpret the shifts and turnings of a single story or saying in its movement across the canon, I take up a current example of "incremental history" and show how it actually works. The example derives from the newest generation, the work of an autodidact. So I cannot be accused of calling up ghosts or invoking long-repudiated approaches to refute an abandoned theory. What I think becomes clear is that the theory I call "incremental history," is "talmudic" in the worst sense. That is, it is ad hoc and made up, just as the Talmud itself makes up history to explain several versions of one saying. Indeed, for all its claim to think in fresh and free ways, the newest generation, as represented here, botches the work. In its bungling, the latest Talmudic historians, as exemplified in Chapter Fifteen, display an intellectual incompetence rarely matched in the earlier, in other ways more credulous and more primitive age of learning.

So, in all, I insist that we begin with facts, appropriately classified and categorized, properly analyzed, explicitly and articulated interpreted. In the conclusion I simply point to what has now to be done. That, in a few words, is the thesis and method of this book.

To introduce the exercises that are to follow, let me begin with a comparison of a single passage as it makes its way from Mekhilta, generally thought to be an early composition of exegeses of Scripture, to the Tosefta, thence to the Yerushalmi, and finally to the Bavli. Here we see precisely how the sages who received a piece of composition proposed to preserve the given but also to transmit something new. The passage at hand complements M. Hag. 2:1-2, which refers to a corpus of doctrine

connected to Ezekiel's vision of the chariot (Ez. Ch. 1). In the left-hand column, I present
the matter as it occurs in the Mekhilta attributed to R. Simeon. In the next, I give the
Tosefta's version, in the third, the Yerushalmi's, and in the fourth, the Bavli's.

Mekhilta de R. Simeon	Tos. Hag 2:1-2	Y. Hag. 2:1	B. Hag. 14b
And the story is told that Yohanan was riding on an ass and going out of Jerusalem	(see Mekhilta de R. Simeon)	(see Mekhilta de R. Simeon) going on the way riding on an ass	Teno Rabbanan The story is told that Yohanan was riding an ass and going on the way, and Eleazar was
Eleazar b. Arakh his disciple was going behind him.	Driving the ass	going	driving the ass
Eleazar: Teach me a chapter in the Merkavah	(see Mekhilta de R. Simeon)	(see Mekhilta de R. Simeon)	(see Mekhilta de R. Simeon)
Yohanan: Have I not taught you. Not of the Merkavah.... understand of his own knowledge.	told	see Mekhilta de R. Simeon)	taught
If not, give me permission to speak before you.	(see Mekhilta de R. Simeon)	(see Mekhilta de R. Simeon)	before you something you taught me.
	Yohanan descended from the ass, covered self with cloak; both sat on a stone under an olive tree.	Yohanan descended saying, It is not lawful that I should hear the glory of my creator and be riding on an ass. They went and sat under the tree.	Forthwith Yohanan descended from the ass, covered himself, and sat on the stone under the olive-tree.
			He said to him, Rabbi, why did you descend.

			He said to him, Is it possible that you should expound the Chariot, and the Shekhinah be with us, and the ministering angels accompany us, and I should ride an ass?
Eleazar expounded until flames licked around about.	He lectured before him.	Forthwith all the trees broke out in song and said Ps. 96.	Eleazar opened on the Chariot and expounded, and fire went down from heaven and encompassed all the trees roundabout. What song did the trees sing? Ps. 145.
			An angel answered from the fire and said, These, these are the works of the chariot.
When Yohanan saw the flames, he got off the ass, kissed him, and said.	He stood and kissed him and said, Blessed is the Lord God of Israel who gave a son to Abraham our father who knows how to understand and expound the glory of his father in heaven. Some expound well but do not fulfill well, and vice versa, but but Eleazar does both well.	When Eleazar finished the Works of the Chariot, Yohanan stood and kissed him on his head and said,	Yohanan stood up and kissed him on his head and said, Blessed is the Lord, God of Israel who gave a son to Abraham our father who knows how to understand and to investigate, and to expound the Chariot.
Eleazar, Happy she that bore you. Happy Abraham our father that such has come forth from his loins.		Blessed is the Lord, God of Abraham. Jacob who gave to Abraham a son wise and knowing how to expound the glory of our father in	Some preach well, etc.

heaven. Some preach well... Eleazar does both well.

Happy are you Abraham our father that Eleazar has come forth from your loins.

Happy are you, Abraham our father that Eleazar b. Arakh has come forth from your loins, who knows how to understand and expound the glory of his father in heaven.

Happy are you, Abraham our father, that Eleazar has come forth from your loins.

He would say, If all sages were on one side of the scale and Eleazar on the other, he would outweigh them all.

R. Yose b. Judah: Joshua lectured before Yohanan, ᶜAqiba before Joshua, Hananiah b. Hakhinai before ᶜAqiba.

When Joseph the priest and Simeon b. Natanel heard, they too opened a discourse on the on the Chariot.

They said, it was, the first day of summer, and the earth trembled, and a rainbow appeared and an echo came and said to them, Behold the place is ready for you and your disciples are slated for the third class.

And when these things were told to Joshua, he and Yose the priest were walking on the way. They said Let us also expound the Chariot. Joshua opened and expounded. That day was the first day of summer, but the heavens clouded over and a kind of a rainbow appeared, and the angels gathered and came to hear like men running to a wedding.

Joshua and Yose the priest went and told these things to Yohanan, who said, Happy are you, and

happy are those who
bore you. Happy are
my eyes who have
seen such.

And also you and I
in my dream were
reclining on Mount
Sinai and an echo
came forth to us
from heaven, "Come
up hither, come up
hither. Your dis-
ciples are slated
for the third class.

Is this so? And is
it not taught?
(TNY'):

Joshua laid out
matters before Yoh-
anan, Aqiba before
Joshua, Hananiah b.
Hakhinai before
Aqiba.

And Eleazar is not
mentioned.

It would be difficult to invent a better example of the development of a tradition from simplicity to complexity, from being relatively unadorned to being full articulated, and from earlier to later versions. In the earliest document the story is shortest, simplest. The Tosefta represents an obvious expansion. The Palestinian Talmudic account is still further enriched with details and entirely new components. And the Babylonian version, last of all and youngest in the age of the document in which it appears, clearly is most fully, carefully worked out. The Mekhilta's components are:

1.   Yohanan riding an ass
2.   Eleazar with him
3.   Teach me -- It is illegal.
4.   Then let me speak.
5.   Eleazar expounded and flames licked round about.

6.   Then Yohanan blessed him, Your mother and Abraham are happy.

7.   Scale

The concluding element (No. 7) is, as I said, a separate and unrelated saying. It plays no integral part whatever in the Merkavah tradition.

The Tosefta's version is close to the foregoing, but it adds that Yohanan ceremoniously descended from the ass before the lecture began. Only then did Eleazar say his sermon. The detail about the flames, on the other hand, is absent. But the blessing is greatly expanded. The praise is now extended to Eleazar's ability to achieve a fully realized mystic experience; he does not merely describe the Merkavah, but presumably is able to go down in it. Then a second, and separate, blessing is repeated from Mekhilta, Happy are you... This clearly indicates dependence, for the first blessing would be sufficient in an independent account. But the second blessing is augmented with reference to the Mekhilta's: Abraham should be happy because you expound well and fulfill well. Thus the narrator tied in the duplicated blessing of the original version. The most important omission is the praise of Eleazar. This is replaced by the story that Joshua did the same before Yohanan, Aqiba afterward, and so forth. the later version thus emphasized that despite the excellence of Eleazar, which no one denied, the true line of transmission extended through Joshua, not through Eleazar. We may assume the first and simplest version derives from Eleazar's school, and the second has been altered, then handed on in the Joshua-Aqiba line.

The Palestinian version begins as do the early ones. But it adds a careful explanation of why Yohanan got off the ass. This explanation is itself rather fulsome. Only afterward do the master and disciple sit down -- under a tree, the olive is lost. Then fire comes down, but this detail, from the Mekhilta version, is greatly embellished. Angels dance as at a wedding. They even praise Eleazar's sermon, before Yohanan has a chance to say anything. He plays no part in the proliferating details. Then the trees sing a Psalm. Only after the expanded element has been completed do we return to the matter of Yohanan. He then kisses Eleazar and gives the double blessing. Blessed is the Lord... Happy are you, Abraham. Then Joseph/Yose the priest and Simeon are introduced, with further supernatural events accompanying their never-recorded sermon. The echo invites them to the third level of the heavens.

The Babylonian version is augmented in almost every detail. Eleazar is not merely walking, but driving the ass. He wants to teach something he has already heard. Not only does Yohanan descend, but Eleazar asks why he did so. This is clearly a point at which the Babylonian version has expanded on a mute detail in the immediately preceding account. Yohanan then develops his earlier saying. It is not merely the glory of the creator, but rather both the Shekhinah and the Ministering angels are present. Eleazar speaks, and fire pours from heaven. The trees sing a Psalm, this time Ps. 145. An angel repeats the message of the Palestinian version. The order of the trees' psalm and the angels message is therefore reversed. Then comes the kiss -- now on his head -- and the blessing is expanded to include to investigate after to understand and to expound. The Some preach well formula comes verbatim, then the second blessing. Joshua is now the link. The story is drawn from the earlier version. The rainbow is not enough; now the angels come to a wedding -- a detail presumably borrowed from the Palestinian dance of the ministering angels. Then Yose told Yohanan, who expressed approval. The heavenly echo of the Palestinian version becomes the whole dream about the circle of Yohanan on Mount Sinai, with a direct invitation to heaven, both elements based upon and developments of Behold the place is ready for you.

As I said, I can think of no better demonstration of the fact that versions of a single story appearing in documents of successive age normally proceed from the simpler to the more complex formulation as they pass from an earlier document to a later one. Since they clearly depend on one another, there can be no question as to which comes first, which later, in time of formulation. If I may now generalize on the basis of the demonstration at hand: the framers of the Bavli clearly proposed to contribute their own, original ideas to a received tradition. What they wished to do, it further is clear, is to rewrite and revise to suit their tastes about what a full and conclusive account of the matter required.

A single example does not constitute a proof, of course. I cannot say precisely what sort of sample of the whole would be required to establish the simple, but critical claim at hand concerning the Bavli's editorial policies and program. One important aspect is whether the same relationship that the Bavli's authors establish to the materials presented to them in the Yerushalmi characterizes their approach to other documents. A second is to see the somewhat more complex interplay among three documents, one of them the Bavli. A third is to ask whether the Bavli's authors find themselves constrained by the details of what the Yerushalmi's authors in particular set down or whether they were prepared to make fundamental changes in the received materials. A fourth is to inquire about whether attribution to Tannaite authority is one of the Talmuds means that a passage enjoyed more protection from the hands of the artists of the Bavlie than the absence of such an attribution. We proceed to take up examples pertinent to each of these questions in turn.

From the Yerushalmi to The Fathers According to Rabbi Nathan to the Bavli

In the following exercise, we take up four versions of the death-scene of Yohanan ben Zakkai, two occurring in the Yerushalmi, one in the Fathers according to Rabbi Nathan, a document secondary to Mishnah-tractate Abot ("The Fathers"), and, finally, the Bavli's version of the same matter.

Y. A.Z. 3:1	Y. Sot. 9:16	ARNa Ch. 25	B. Ber. 28b
R. Jacob b. Idi in the name of R. Joshua b. Levi	(see y. A.Z. 3:1)	---	Teno Rabbanan When Eleazar was dying, his disciples came to visit...

When Yohanan was dying, he said	commanded and said	---	And when Yohanan fell ill, his disciples came to visit. When he saw them, he wept.
---	---	When Yohanan was dying, he raised his voice and wept.	
---	---	Disciples said, Tall pillar, light of the world, mighty hammer why weep?	Disciples said Light of Israel, Right-hand pillar, Mighty hammer Why weep?
---	---	Do I go to judgment before a mortal kind, who dies and can be bribed? I go before king of kings and don't know his decision Ps. 22:30	If I were going before mortal king who may be bribed, I'd weep. Now that I go before immortal God, and do not know his decision, should I not weep?
---	---	---	They said, Bless us. He said, May you fear heaven as much as you fear men.
Clear the house because of uncleanness	clear the courtyard	---	When he died, he said, Clear out the vessels and prepare a chair for Hezekiah who comes.
And give a chair for Hezekiah king of Judah	ordain		
Rabbi Eliezer when dying said	---	---	---

Clear the house
because of un-
cleanness   ---   ---   ---

And set a chair for
Rabban Yohanan
ben Zakkai   ---   ---   ---

The two Palestinian Talmudic versions are simple and unadorned. That in y. A.Z. 3:1
includes the death scene of Eliezer, but in proper chronological order, that is, first
Yohanan, then Eliezer. The reference to a chair for Yohanan is omitted in the corre-
sponding death scene in Ber. 28b, which is as different for Eliezer as it is for Yohanan. Y.
Sot. 9:16 omits all reference to Eliezer's death scene. It is otherwise close to the account
of Jacob b. Idi in Joshua's name in Y. A.Z., and is given the same attribution. The long
beraita in b. Ber. 28b involves an extended account of Eliezer's death, followed by a
similarly long version of Yohanan's. The "clear out the vessels," which is the point of the
Palestinian versions, is rather awkwardly tacked on at the end by the device of having the
long sermon introduced by When he was sick, and the dying words by In the hour of his
death. The final blessing is included, parallel to that of Eliezer, but of different content.
The ARNa version omits all reference to Eliezer. It begins with Yohanan's weeping; the
disciples play a less important role; and they do not get a blessing at the end. Light of
Israel becomes of the world; right-hand pillar becomes tall pillar; that is, the Babylonian
version is more specific alludes to concrete images. The actual homilies require closer
comparison:

ARNa	B. Ber. 28b
Do I go before a king of flesh and blood	If I went before a king of flesh and
- whose anger is of this world	blood, who is here today and in the
- whose punishment is of this	grave tomorrow
world	- whose anger is not eternal
- whose death-penalty is of this	- whose imprisonment is not eternal
world	- whose death-penalty is not eternal
- who can be bribed with words or	And I can bribe him with words or
money?	money
	Even so would I weep
	I go before the eternal God
I go before King of Kings	- whose anger is eternal
- whose anger is eternal	- whose imprisonment is eternal
- who cannot be bribed with words	- whose death-penalty is eternal
or money	

Before me are two roads, one to Paradise, one to Gehenna	And before me are two roads, one to Paradise, one to Gehenna
And I do not know to which he will sentence me.	And I do not know to which one he will sentence me.
And of this the verse says -- Ps. 22:30.	Should I not weep?
	They said to him, Master, bless us?
	[As above.]

The homilies are practically identical, certainly close enough to show dependence on one another. It is therefore striking that the concluding blessing is absent in ARNa. I think the additional clause in the Bavli's version was added so that Yohanan's death-scene would be symmetrical to Eliezer's. The same factor accounts for the importance of the disciples in the beraita's death-scene, by contrast to their role as mere bystanders in ARNa.

It seems clear to me that the primary Palestinian version is y. A.Z. 3:1, for it is unlikely that Jacob b. Idi in Joshua's name would have handed on two separate versions, on long, the other short. Rather the Y. Sot. 9:16 version has merely been shortened by the omission of reference to Eliezer. It is otherwise so close as to be completely dependent on the longer version. There can be no question of relative age. Both appear in the name of the same master and cannot be thought to come from different schools or periods.

The Babylonian and ARNa versions are another matter. I should imagine, following the former analogy, that b. Ber. 28b is the older, more complete version, shaped along the lines of Eliezer's death scene, as I said. ARNa afterward omits the details involving masters other than Yohanan, introduces the exegesis of Ps. 22:30, and concludes with the (probably) famous, "Clear the house..."

What are the primary elements of Yohanan's death scene? Clearly they began with "Clear the house... prepare a chair," which appears throughout, even to the point of being awkwardly tacked on in b. Ber. 28b and ARNa. In the Palestinian accounts, by contrast, the two-fold message fits together without strain. In the ARNa and B. Ber. versions, we thus find five further, certainly later elements:

1. He wept as he was sick/dying,
2. Disciples [came to visit and] asked why,
3. And heaped on him encomia,
4. He replied saying he was going to eternal judgment and did not know the likely decision,
5. [They asked to be blessed].

I see no reason to suppose all these elements are not late inventions, coming long after the very simple account of Joshua b. Levi. They cannot be called "expansions" of Joshua's account; indeed they bear little or no relationship to it. Rather they make use of some of the same materials as Joshua, particularly the Clear the house... set a chair... These may not have been original with Joshua. We do not have to imagine the Bavli's version was shaped by masters who had ever even heard Joshua's version. Indeed, I doubt they did.

To conclude: The death-scene went from the simple to the complex, and from the Palestinian Talmud's attribution by R. Jacob b. Idi to R. Joshua, on the other hand, to the fully articulated beraita-form (Teno Rabbanan) on the other. ARNa again seems closer to the Babylonian beraita than to the simpler Palestinian version. It seems to me possible that the question of the date of the ARNa will have to be restudied, for it sometimes conforms not to the earlier Palestinian versions, but to the substantially later Babylonian ones. Even though all authorities derive from the third century or earlier, the forms of important sayings which do exhibit Babylonian parallels normally adhere to those Babylonian parallels, hence to later, Babylonian developments of Palestinian materials or to materials invented to begin with in the Babylonian schools.

We once again see clearly that a passage frequently shows development and elaboration when it appears in later documents, with the Bavli at the end of the line more often than not. Details are added later on. As we follow stories through several recensions, we do find that passages are normally developed, details are added, and, as I said, the Bavli's version commonly is the fullest and best elaborated.

From the Sifre on Deuteronomy to the Bavli

Sifre Deut. 144	B. San. 32b
Righteousness... shall pursue	Teno Rabbanan
	Righteousness... shall pursue.
Go after a good court.	Go after a good court.
After the court of Yohanan.	After the court of Eliezer in Lud
After the court of Eliezer.	After the court Yohanan in Beror Hayil
	Teno Rabbanan
	Righteousness... shall pursue
	Go after the sages to the academy
	[yeshivah].
	After Eliezer to Lud
	After Yohanan to Beror Hayil
	After Joshua to Peqiin
	After Gamaliel to Yavneh
	After Aqiva to Bnei Beraq
	After Matthew to Rome
	After Hananiah b. Teradion to Sikhnin
	After Yose to Sepphoris
	After Judah b. Bathyra to Nisibis

> After Hananiah nephew of R. Joshua to
> the Exile
> After Rabbi [Judah] to Bet Shearim
> After the sages to the Hewn Stone
> Chamber.

The two versions appear in sequence in the Babylonian Talmud. The latter of the two obviously is an expansion of the former, the brief and simple version of Sifre Deut. It adds the details of where their courts were. I think it unlikely that, had those details been at first included, they would later on have been suppressed. It would have deprived the disciples of useful information, and there was no good reason to do so. The third and longest entry cannot date from the earlier than the first third of the third century. We see the immense expansion of the one quoted just above. Eliezer and Yohanan keep their places. Then follows the first generation of Yavneh, that is, Joshua and Gamaliel; then the generation of Aqiba; then the one immediately following the Bar Kokhba war; finally Judah; and at the end, "the sages" to the (presumably eschatological) Hewn Stone chamber. It is again noteworthy that the versions appearing in later documents are elaborated and clearly later than the versions appearing in earlier documents.

From the Yerushalmi to Bavli

We come now to two simple instances in which materials occur in the Yerushalmi and then in the Bavli, with no intervening stage (if that is what the Fathers according to Rabbi Nathan represents) and little complexity.

The Mishnah states that if one is coming along the way and hears an outcry and says, "May it be his will that this does not come from my house," that is a false prayer. We then find the following:

> He was coming from the way, what does he say? "I am sure that these
> are not in my house."
> Hillel the Elder says, "From a bad report he does not fear." (Ps. 112:7).

The next version is attributed to Tannaim, with the redactional superscription. Our rabbis taught (Teno rabbanan), then given a duplicated superscription, story about (Maaseh b). It follows:

> Hillel the Elder was coming from a journey, and he heard the sound of an
> outcry in the city. He said, "I am sure this is not my house."
> And of him Scripture says, "From a bad report he does not fear: his
> heart is steadfast, trusting in the Lord (Ps. 112:7)."

Hillel's "exegesis" of Ps. 112:7 thus is turned into a story. The verse of Scripture cited concerning Hillel is made to say in the second story what anyone is supposed to say according to the first version. I take it for granted that the Bavli's version comes later than, is and is based upon, the Palestinian Talmudic version (which is not given a Tannaitic attribution!). The word-for-word correspondences make this virtually certain, and the movement from an anonymous to a named teaching seems to me decisive evidence that the Babylonian version depends upon the Palestinian.

The second story bears attribution, in the Bavli's version, to Tannaite authority. While such an attribution is commonly interpreted to mean that the story derives from authorities who occur, also, in the Mishnah and hence from the second century or before, the example at hand will not sustain that theory of the matter. From the present perspective that is a tangential point. The main thing, once more, is simply to see what the Bavli is prepared to do with materials first used in the Yerushalmi. In the present exercise, however, I list the Bavli first, then the Yerushalmi, to show that the result remains the same, however we arrange the sources. We begin with the texts under study.

A. Our rabbis taught (TNW RBNN): The story is told about (M'SH B) a certain man whose sons did not conduct themselves in a proper manner. He arose and wrote his estate over to Jonathan b. Uzziel.
What did Jonathan b. Uzziel do? He sold a third, consecrated a third, and returned a third to his sons [of the man].

B. Shammai came upon him with his staff and bag.
He said to him, "Shammai, if you can take back what I have sold and what I have consecrated, you can also take back what I have returned. But if not, neither can you take back what I have returned."

C. He exclaimed, "The son of Uzziel has confounded me, the son of Uzziel has confounded me."

B. Baba Batra 133b-134a,
(trans. I.W. Slotki, 562)

The setting is supplied by a saying of Samuel to Judah not to transfer inheritances even from bad sons to good ones. What is even more interesting is the following story, which concerns the disciples of Hillel: The greatest of them was Jonathan, the least was Yohanan ben Zakkai. So the framework is set of pericopae on the greatness of Jonathan b. Uzziel, and the above story is, with interruptions and glosses, in fact part of a little Jonathan b. Uzziel-tractate.

The story seems to be a unity, but only if it depends on Y. Ned. 5:6. Otherwise, part B is certainly separate, for we have no hint of Shammai's involvement in part A. Here is the Yerushalmi's version:

A. Said Rabbi Yose b. Rabbi Bun, "Thus was the case ['BD']: 'Jonathan b. Uzziel's father foreswore him from his property, and arose and wrote them over to Shammai.'

B. "'What did Shammai do? He sold part, sanctified part, and gave the rest to him [Jonathan] as a gift, and said, 'Whoever will come and complain against this gift, let him remove the hand of the purchasers and from the hand of the sanctuary and afterward he may remove from his hand.'"

Y. Nedarim 5:6

The Palestinian version of the Jonathan-story is strikingly different from the Babylonian beraita. Here the gift is to Shammai, who acts in behalf of Jonathan by saving for him part of the father's property. Shammai's presence is now comprehensible. This is the whole pericope. The story certainly is a unitary composition. No element comes as a surprise; nothing is intruded. Now to the comparison:

B. B.B. 133b-134a	Y. Ned. 5:6
1. TNW RBNN	1. R. Yose b. R. Bun said
2. Ma'aseh b-	2. Thus was the thing ('BD')
3. One man whose sons did not behave according to rule.	3. ---
4. He rose and wrote his property to Jonathan b. Uzziel	4. Jonathan b . Uzziel's father prevented him by vow from his property and rose and wrote them to Shammai.
5. What did Jonathan b. Uzziel do?	5. What did Shammai do?
6. He sold a third	6. He sold part
7. consecrated a third	7. consecrated part
8. and returned a third to his sons.	8. and gave him the rest as a gift.
9. Shammai came to him in his staff and bag.	9. ---
10. He said to him, Shammai, if you can take away what I have sold and what I have consecrated, you can take away what I have returned.	10. He [Shammai] said, Whoever will come and complain against this gift, let him retrieve from the hand of the sanctuary, and afterward let him remove from the hand of this one.
11. If not, you cannot take away what I have returned.	11. [As above]
12. He said, Ben Uzziel has confounded me [twice].	12. ---

One version completely reverses the account of the other. The first question is, Which comes first? It seems to me that the Palestinian version absolutely must precede the Babylonian beraita, and that the latter certainly had to have been shaped in complete dependency upon it. Why so sure? The decisive fact is the intrusion of Shammai into the Babylonian version in no. 9. Who mentioned his name? Only in the Palestinian version is Shammai integral to the story. One could, to be sure, divide the beraita into fragments of two independent stories, one in which Jonathan b. Uzziel plays the major, and affirmative role, the other in which Shammai somehow is brought into play. But that theoretical division seems to me unlikely, in the face of the fact that the Palestinian account supplies a complete and unitary story. Both parties there play a part from the outset. No one has to be intruded afterward.

The Babylonian version has translated 'BD' into its conventional superscription, ma'aseh b. It has supplied the reason for the disinheritance. In the Palestinian version we understand at the very outset why Jonathan was included -- it was his own father. In the Babylonian, we are as mystified by the fight to Jonathan as by the intrusion of Shammai.

The Babylonian concretizes <u>part</u> to <u>third,</u> obvious but still an improvement. The action of Shammai in the Palestinian version is now copied by Jonathan in the other. Since Shammai is involved in the Palestinian one, the Babylonians have to invent a dramatic encounter to bring in Shammai. Now "whoever will come" is turned into "Shammai, if you." The elements of no. 10 are otherwise not much different. The beraita is somewhat more fluent: if you can do this, you can do that and if you cannot do this, you cannot do that. The Palestinian has thus been improved by the division into affirmative and negative clauses, thus making a binding condition, and the references to hand of purchasers/sanctuary are turned into active verbs. The absence of no. 12 in the Palestinian version is for obvious reasons. So the Babylonian version is certainly later than the Palestinian one.

From Josephus to the Bavli

Since Josephus wrote his works in Aramaic, then having them translated into Greek, we may hardly be surprised to find in rabbinic documents familiarity with materials also known to us in the writings of Josephus. To begin with, let us first deal with the relevant passages as they occur in the rabbinic canon, then turn to Josephus' version of the same matters. There are two important passages, one in the Tosefta, the other in the Bavli. The former serves to establish the fact that exactly the same words occur in both a rabbinic composition, Tos. Sotah 13:7, and Josephus' narrative. The latter then shows clear and unmistakable dependence of the Talmudic version of a story upon Josephus' version of the same story.

> Yohanan the High Priest heard from the house of the Holy of Holies,
> <u>"The young men who went out to make war against Antioch have conquered"</u>
> and they noted that hour, and it tallied that they had conquered at that very hour.

The italicized words are in Aramaic, the rest in Hebrew. The point of the pericope is a miraculous revelation to Yohanan, another indication of the high favor he enjoyed in rabbinical circles. The kernel of the pericope is the Aramaic passage, in which case the point must be as given, that Yohanan was vouchsafed a heavenly revelation. The Bavli's story of importance in our inquiry is as follows:

A. Abbaye said, "How do I know it [re the silence of a husband in a case in which the wife is charged with committing adultery by one witness only, that the husband must divorce the wife if he remains silent]?"

B. DTNY': The story is told that (M'SH B) Yannai the King went to Kohalit in the wilderness and there conquered sixty towns. When he returned, he rejoiced greatly, and invited all the sages of Israel.

C. He said to them, "Our forefathers would eat salt fish when they were engaged in the building of the Holy House. Let us also eat salt fish as a memorial to our forefathers."

D. So they brought up salt fish on golden tables, and they ate.

E. There was there a certain scoffer, evil-hearted and empty headed, and Eleazar ben Po'irah was his name.

F. Eleazar b. Po'irah said to Yannai the king, "O King Yannai, the hearts of the Pharisees are [set] against you."

G. "What shall I do?"

H. "Test (HQM) them by the plate (SYS) that is between your eyes."

I. He tested them by the plate that was between his eyes.

J. There was there a certain sage, and Judah b. Gedidiah was his name. Judah b. Gedidiah said to Yannai the King, "O King Yannai, Let suffice for you the crown of sovereignty [kingship]. Leave the crown of the [high] priesthood for the seed of Aaron."

K. For people said that his [Yannai's] mother had been taken captive in Modiim. The charge was investigated and not found [sustained]. The sages of Israel departed in anger.

L. Eleazar b. Po'irah then said to Yannai the king, "O King Yannai, That is the law [not here specified as the punishment inflicted on Judah] even for the ordinary folk in Israel. But you are king and high priest -- should that be your law too?"

M. "What should I do?"

N. "If you take my advice, you will trample them down."

O. "But what will become of the Torah?"

P. "Lo, it is rolled up and lying in the corner. Whoever wants to learn, let him come and learn."

Q. R. Nahman b. Isaac said, "<u>Forthwith Epicureanism [^CPYQWRSWT] was instilled in him [Yannai], for he should have said, 'That is well and good for the Written Torah, but what will become of the Oral Torah?'</u>" [In Aramaic.]

R. The evil blossomed through Eleazar b. Po'irah. All the sages of Israel were killed.

S. The world was desolate until Simeon b. Shetah came and restored the Torah to its place.

B. Qid.66a

A persistent tradition on a falling out between the Pharisees and Alexander Jannaeus evidently circulated in later times. One form of that tradition placed the origin of the whole difficulty at the feet of Simeon b. Shetah himself, holding that the king believed he had been cheated; therefore Simeon fled for a time but later on returned. A second, and different, set of traditions, of which the above is one exemplum, held that difficulties between Yannai and the Pharisees ("rabbis") as a group led to the flight of many of them, including Judah b. Tabbai and/or Joshua b. Perahiah to Alexandria. Simeon managed to patch things up -- we do not know how -- and therefore summoned the refugees to return. But the two traditions cannot be reconciled or translated into historical language, nor can we profitably speculate on what 'kernel' of historical truth underlay either or both of them. All we do know is that Simeon b. Shetah was believed to have played a role in either the difficulty, or the reconciliation, or both.

This brings us to Josephus' versions of both items. They occur in the account of John Hyrcanus (135-104), first in War I:54ff. He succeeded his murdered brothers as high priest and led the state for thirty-one years (1:68). He enjoyed the "three highest privileges: the supreme command of the nation, the high priesthood, and the gift of prophecy. He could invariably predict the future." In the pertinent materials in the War, Josephus makes no mention of Pharisees. In Antiquities XIII, Josephus vastly expands his account. He credits John Hyrcanus with the destruction of the Gerizim temple and the conversion of Idumaea (13:2524). The heavenly message now appears as follows:

> Now about the high priest Hyrcanus an extraordinary story is told, how the Deity communicated with him, for they say that on the very day on which his sons fought with Cyzicenus, Hyrcanus, who was alone in the Temple, burning incense as high priest, heard a voice saying that his sons had just defeated Antiochus. And on coming out of the Temple, he revealed this to the entire multitude, and so it actually happened.

The message here preserved in indirect discourse is presented in direct discourse in the rabbinic materials: "The youths who have made war on Antioch have conquered." But the message is nearly identical, and so is the setting.

Josephus now introduces the story of the Pharisees and Hyrcanus (13:288ff., trans. L.H. Feldman):

> As for Hyrcanus, the envy of the Jews was aroused against him by his own successes, and those of his sons. Particularly hostile to him were the Pharisees, who are one of the Jewish schools... And so great is their influence with the masses that even when they speak against a high or high priest, they immediately gain credence.

> Hyrcanus too was a disciple of theirs, and was greatly loved by them. And once he invited them to a feast and entertained them hospitably, and when he saw that they were having a very good time, he began by saying that they knew he wished to be righteous and in everything he did tried to please God and them -- for the Pharisees profess such beliefs; at the same time he begged them, if they observed him doing anything wrong or straying from the right path, to lead him back to it and correct him. But they testified to his being altogether virtuous, and he was delighted with their praise.

> However, one of his guests, named Eleazar, who had an evil nature and took pleasure in dissension, said, "Since you have asked to be told the truth, if you wish to be righteous give up the high priesthood and be content with governing the people."

> And when Hyrcanus asked him for what reason he should give up the high priesthood, he replied, "Because we have heard from our elders that your mother was a captive in the reign of Antiochus Epiphanes."

But the story was false, and Hyrcanus was furious with the man, while all the Pharisees were very indignant.

Then a certain Jonathan, one of Hyrcanus' close friends, belonging to the school of Sadducees, who hold opinions opposed to those of the Pharisees, said that it had been with general approval of all the Pharisees that Eleazar had made his slanderous statement; and this, he added, would be clear to Hyrcanus if he inquired of them what punishment Eleazar deserved for what he had said.

Hyrcanus did so, and the Pharisees replied: Eleazar deserved stripes and chains; for they did not think it right to sentence a man to death for calumny, and the Pharisees are naturally lenient in the matter of punishments.

Hyrcanus was outraged, and Jonathan in particular inflamed his anger, and so worked upon him that he brought him to join the Sadducean party and desert the Pharisees and to abrogate the regulations which they had established for the people and punish those who observed them.

At this point, Josephus explains who the Pharisees are and alleges that everyone listens to them, while the Sadducees are followed only by the wealthy (etc.). Then Josephus returns to the account of War. Hyrcanus lived happily ever after and had the three greatest privileges, etc.

Clearly, the rabbis' tradition of Alexander Jannaeus at b. Qid. 66a and Josephus' story of John Hyrcanus in Antiquities exhibit remarkable affinities. On Abbaye's theory that Yannai and Yohanan were one and the same, we have no difficulties whatever, and it is Abbaye who cites the materials in b. Qid. 66a.

I am impressed by the near-identity of the miracle-story with the rabbinical one, even more impressed by the antiquity of the language attributed to the heavenly echo, and would be inclined to imagine that to both Josephus and the rabbis was available a single, brief logion in Aramaic. The parallels certainly are too close to be accidental.

The long story about Hyrcanus (=b. Qid.'s Jannaeus) and the Pharisees is another matter. It is long, well developed, and involves not a single short phrase, but a complex narrative. Josephus has inserted it whole into his larger setting. He does not account for Pharisaic hostility, but takes it for granted; then he makes Hyrcanus a Pharisee, so their hostility is even more incredible. Now comes the famous banquet, with Eleazar (= Judah b. Gedidiah of the Talmud) as the trouble-maker, described with much the same adjectives, and his message is identical in substance. Everyone "leaves indignant" in both versions. Then Jonathan (the Talmud's Eleazar b. Po'irah) tells the king to let the Pharisees show their true feelings. They impose the normal punishment. This detail is absent in b. Qid. 66a. But it is there taken for granted. That is striking indeed. "That is the law even for the most humble... shall that be your law too?" follows the departure of the sages. Let me state with appropriate emphasis: <u>The version in b. Qid. 66a, if not garbled or defective, therefore is incomprehensible without the details supplied in Josephus' story</u>. Now Josephus explains how Hyrcanus left the Pharisees and joined the Sadducees, after which he lived happily. This detail ignores the foregoing narrative. For the rabbis the break came on the threshold of his death and is left unexplained. Then Simeon b. Shetah comes along and restores the Pharisees to power.

I find it impossible to imagine how the two versions could have been shaped independently of one another. Two facts seem to me decisive. The first is the length and complexity of the narrative, the second, the constant parallels of theme, development, and detail, between the two versions. The two cannot be thought entirely separate traditions, but, on the contrary, may be best accounted for within one of three theories: either Josephus here cites an ancient pre-rabbinic, Pharisaic story (highly unlikely); or both refer in common to a third, independent source; or the rabbis cite Josephus. This third seems to me most probable, if in fact rabbis knew Josephus' writings in the original Aramaic. The upshot is that the Bavli's authors took over and shaped in their own framework materials of a quite elaborate character.

The Bavli at the End

For the present purpose the point is simple. The Bavli consistently takes up materials available to us in sources brought to closure earlier. It does with these materials pretty much the same thing. That is to add details and to provide a sense of the whole -- its purpose, its message -- in so doing. So the Bavli's authors imposed the mark of their own minds upon received materials. They did so in such a way as to revise everything that had gone before. They placed upon the whole heritage of the past the indelible and distinct, unmistakable stamp of their own minds. The reason is that the Bavli's authorities did not confuse respect with servility. They carefully nurtured critical and creative faculties. Gibbon said (probably unfairly) of the Byzantine schools, "Not a single composition of history, philosophy, or literature has been saved from oblivion by the intrinsic beauties of style, or sentiment, or original fancy, or even of successful imita-tion." By contrast, the Bavli is the product not of servility to the past or of dogmatism in the present, but of an exceptionally critical, autonomous rationalism and an utterly independent spirit. The writers gave to pedantry a cool welcome. The authority of the received materials was set aside by the critical judgment of the newest generation. In the fullest sense, the Bavli's authors were not traditionalists. They took traditions of the early generations into their care, respectfully learning them, reverently handing them on. But these they thoroughly digested and made their own. Their minds were filled with the learning of the ancients. But their unrelenting criticism were wholly their own, which is why they added, changed, and rewrote nearly everything they received from, hence shared with, earlier compositions. It follows that the Bavli's changes testify to the intellect of the Bavli's authors.

PART TWO

THE THRICE-TOLD TALE IN
RABBINIC STORIES ABOUT
PHARISEES BEFORE 70

CHAPTER TWO
SIMEON THE JUST

1. Sayings Attributed to Simeon the Just

In the first classification is only one saying of apophthegmatic character, Avot 1:3 (2):

Abot 1:3(2)	Y. Ta. 4:2	Y.Meg.3:6	Pes. de R. Kahana
1. Simeon the Just was among the remnants of the Great Assembly.	1. TMN TNNYN " " "	1. " " "	1. " " " remnants of the <u>whole law</u> (KL HYLKTH)
2. He would say, On three things the world stands, On the Torah, and on the cult, and on deeds of loving kindness.	2. " " "	2. " " "	2. -----
3. -----	3. And all three are in one Scripture, Is. 51	3. " " "	3. -----

Clearly the Abot saying was accurately quoted in the third century, with the addition of an appropriate exegesis, presumably sometime after the Abot-collection was widely available. The version in Pes. de R. Kahana omits the operative moral teaching. The passage probably is garbled. What y. adds is a proof-text.

2. Stories Attributed to Simeon the Just

We have one story told in the name of Simeon the Just about himself. The form is: <u>Simeon the Just said + story told in the first person.</u> When other characters appear in the story, their dialogue is supplied by Simeon.

Sifre Num. 22	Tos. Nez. 4:7
	(Text: S. Lieberman, Tosefta Nasbim [N.Y., 1967] p. 138)

1.	-----	1.	-----
2.	Rabbi Simeon the Just said	2.	" " "[Omits Rabbi]
3.	I never (MWLM) ate the guilt-offering of Naziriteship but one	3.	" " "(MYMYY)
4.	When one came from the south,	4.	Story is told concerning (MSH B) one who came to me from the south
5.	of beautiful eyes, lovely appearance	5.	" " "
6.	and his locks heaped up into curls	6.	" " "
7.	I said (N'M) to him, Quickly must (MHR'YT) one destroy beautiful hair	7.	(NM), My son, Why [What do you see to] destroy this beautiful hair
8.	He said (N'M) to me	8.	(NM) " " "
9.	I was a shepherd in my town	9.	" " "
10.	And I went to fill (ML') water from the well	10.	" " " from the river
11	I looked at my shadow	11.	" " "
12.	and my heart grew haughty (PHZ)	12.	my impulse " " "
13.	It wanted to remove me from the world. (LHBRNY)	13.	" " "
14.	I said (NM) to it, Evil one (RS')	14.	" " "
15.	Lo, you take pride in what is not yours. It belongs to the dust, worm, and maggot.	15.	You had the right to be jealous (GRH) only of something which is not yours, something destined to be made into dust, worm, and maggot.
16.	Lo, I shave you [off] for Heaven. I shaved.	16.	Lo, it is incumbent on me to shave [Omits: I shaved]
17.	Forthwith I kissed him on his head and said (N'M) to him	17.	I bent my head " " "
18.	May such as you increase in Israel, who do the will of the Omnipresent.	18.	My son, " " "
19.	Concerning you is fulfilled	19.	" " "
20.	Num. 6:2	20.	" " "

* * * * *

Y. Ned. 1:1 = Y. Naz. 1:5	B. Naz. 4b = B. Ned. 9a
[Variations in y. Naz. 1:5 in brackets]	

1.	DTNY	1.	TNY'

Y. Ned. 1:1 = Y. Naz. 1:5
[Variations in y. Naz. 1:5 in brackets]

1. DTNY
2. [Omits rabbi]
3. " " "

4. came up to me (LH).
5. I saw him ruddy('DMWNY) with [Naz.: adds DMWT]
6. arranged for him in heaps (TYLY TYLYM) [Naz. omits SDR]
7. " " " my son -- What did you see [= why] destroy this " " "
8. He said (NM) to me, Rabbi [Naz.: NWM']
9. " " "
10. " " " to fill a pail (ML'S'WB) with water
11. I saw (R'H) in the midst of the water
12. my impulse
13. to destroy ('BD) " " "
14. " " "
15. " " "[Omits: It belongs to the

16. It is incumbent on me to sanctify you to heaven
17. " " " [Naz.: I embraced and kissed]
18. " " "

19. Concerning you, Scripture says
20. " " "

B. Naz. 4b = B. Ned. 9a

1. TNY'
2. " " "
3. never (MYMY) -- guilt-offering of an unclean nazir except for one man
4. came to me (B')
5. " " "
6. arranged for him in curls

7. I said (MR') -- my son What did you see to destroy this beautiful hair?
8. " " " ['MR]

9. " " " for my father
10. " " " [to draw, S'B]

11. " " "

12. my impulse " " "
13. to drive me (TWRDNY) '" " "
14. " " " ('MR), Base one (RYQH)
15. On what account do you take pride in the world which is not yours? For your end will be with worm and maggot [Omits: Dust]

16. By the cult [Omits: Lo (HRNY)]

17. I arose and [in place of I shaved]. I said ('MR)
18. May such Nazirites as you [Omits: who do the will ...]

19. Scripture says [Instead of is fulfilled]
20. " " "

The Tosefta stands between the fully revised Babylonian beraita and Sifre Num. Important improvements include the addition of my son (no. 7), this (no. 7), impulse in place of heart (no. 12), and, most striking, the complete revision of no. 15. by which the language is greatly clarified. I have rendered ^CSH in passive, to be made, but it may be translated to make/produce. The unclear shaved my head of no. 16, which is poor diction, is changed to a clause in Simeon's reply, I bent my head. These changes are not fundamental, but superficial and stylistic. The several versions certainly are interdependent. The Palestinian Talmudic versions, which are close to one another, though not identical in all respects, on the whole follow Tosefta, as is to be expected. Story is told of Tos. no. 4 is rightly omitted, but the Yer. versions add several words: ruddy, demut. The oath it is incumbent -- to sanctify occurs, only to be changed in the Babylonian beraita to the exclamatory by the cult. The reference to dust, worm and maggot is omitted in both Palestinian Talmudic versions, perhaps not a lapse of a scribe but a definite literary choice. The most important differences are, in general, between the earliest version and the latest; the intermediate versions are transitional.

The accounts in Sifre Num. and b. Naz. are closely related, for all differences are minor. No major element in one account is omitted in the other. But the beraita consistently supplies details left out of the version of Sifre Num., for instance unclean Nazir, explaining what Simeon the Just had against guilt offerings of Nazirs; came to me, arranged for him)addition of sedurot lo) in curls; my son added to the colloquy. The difficult language of Sifre Num., MHR'YT, which I roughly translated, Quickly must one, is corrected in favor of a much more lucid what did you see [= what made you, why] (i.e. MH R'YT -- not much of a change). The diction is then improved with the addition of this beautiful hair. The shepherd now works for my father. Fill is replaced by draw, which settles the matter of the duplicated verbs in the Palestinian versions (no. 10), where both roots occur. Heart is dropped in favor of impulse (YSR), possibly more colloquial. The change of TRD for BR or 'BD' probably is for the same reason. Like no. 7, no. 15 is improved in the beraita by the inclusion of the more complete and lucid statement, phrased in the form of a question, On what account, followed by a declarative For your end ... All that survives of the Sifre version is the stock-reference to dust, worm, and maggot, and the choice of PHZ and G'H. Similarly in no. 16, the Lo is replaced by the language of a vow, By the cult. In the absence of the oath "by the Temple cult", the force of the vow is diminished; by the cult intensifies lo. The changes in nos. 17 and 18 conform to the earlier ones: I arose and Nazirites add, in the former instance, a more colloquial expression, in the latter, a more pointed reference to the sort of Nazirites Simeon hopes will multiply. The general who do the will is made more specific and precise: Nazirites. The Scripture is set into different citation-form. In Sifre Num. the Scripture is fulfilled in the Nazirite; in the Palestinian and beraita-versions is found the language common in the Babylonian Talmud, "Scripture says concerning you..."

It is difficult to deny that the beraita-version depends, and improves, upon that in Sifre Num. Valuable details are added to the Sifre's account. The language is clarified and in several points is made to conform to rabbinical diction and word-choice. While some of the differences may represent merely different linguistic conventions (N'M/'MR), most of them enhance the Sifre version. The beraita thus comes later than the version in Sifre Num. This dependence is not merely in the general outline of the story; the differences are not in generalities but in minor details. These cannot have been independent accounts which circulated separately; the authority responsible for the beraita seems to have had the Sifre version before him.

The differences between the versions of the beraita in b. Ned. and Naz. are negligible. If Sifre were dated later than the other versions, what we have called improvements would have to be regarded as corruptions of superior, earlier versions.

3. Stories about Simeon the Just

Of the four stories told about, or containing references to, Simeon the Just, two are historical, and two are of a miraculous, or supernatural, character, a distinction the narrator would not have recognized. The former pertain to Simeon's preparing a heifer-sacrifice and to his encounter with Alexander of Macedonia. The latter are, first, the heavenly-message story, and second, the list of supernatural changes in the life of the cult, marking Simeon's death.

a. Heifer

M. Parah 3:5	Y. Sheq. 4:2	Pes. de R. Kahana
1. Who made them?	1. -----	1. -----
2 Simeon the Just and Yohanan the high priest made two each	2. -----	2. -----
3. -----	3. Ulla objected before Mana, Lo it is taught (TNY):	3. ----- [Here: Anonymous] Lo it is taught
4. -----	4. Simeon the Just made two [omits: each]	4. Simeon the Just made two heifers
5. -----	5. He did not bring the second out on the ramp on which he brought out the first	5. [Identical to y. Sheq.]
6. -----	6. Can you say he was wasteful [etc]?	6. Can you say that just man [etc]?

The Mishnah is referred to in the later versions, but not cited verbatim. The reference to Yohanan the High Priest is deliberately omitted. This leaves a lacuna, filled in by the latest midrashic compilation with the addition of heifers. The other change, for he supplying that just man, intensifies the ironic force of the question. TNY means that the editor alludes to the Mishnah. Clearly the later materials depend upon the earlier, but they have also greatly augmented the Mishnah, by supplying the "fact" that the high priests had wastefully constructed the ramp referred to in M. Parah 3:6, "They would construct a ramp from the Temple Mount to the Mount of Olives." The assumption made by the later masters is that for each sacrifice a new ramp was constructed. But this must then apply to all the priests listed in 3:5, including Simeon the Just. The problem is how to distinguish Simeon the Just, a high priest admired by rabbis, from others on that same list, who are not held in high esteem. The later history of the High priesthood is told in lurid colors by Pharisaic-rabbinic tradition. No restraints limited expression of rabbinic hostility against the late priesthood. Hence, if anyone implies all high priests did the same lavish act, Simeon must forthwith be cited to show the act was not disreputable at all.

The inclusion of no. 5 is <u>not</u> part of the citation of the Mishnah, though it occurs under the superscription TNY. I do not know whence the <u>beraita</u> derives, for Tos. Par. 3:7 follows the Mishnah at the pertinent place. The inference that the ramp could not be used twice was drawn from M. Par. 3:5-6, but we do not know who drew it, why, or when it was important to add to the anti-priestly polemic this particular detail. But at that point the problem of Simeon's inclusion in the list had to be faced.

The <u>terminus ante quem</u> is the middle of the third century A.D. Clearly, the detail about the priests' constructing new ramps circulated separately from the Mishnah and was added to the <u>beraita</u> later on. Yet, standing by itself, it is incomprehensible, for a saying <u>Simeon did not bring the second out ...</u> would mean nothing outside of the context of "Simeon the Just made two."

The additional detail of the <u>beraita</u> depended upon the Mishnah, having been added later as a commentary on Mishnah 3:6, as I said. We therefore cannot regard no. 5 as an independent tradition.

b. Alexander

B. Yoma 69a		Lev. R. 13:5	Pes. R. Kahana	Pes. Rabbati
1.	TNY'	1. -----	1. -----	1. -----
2.	Forbidden to mourn on the 25th of Tevet, the day of Mt. Gerizim.	2. -----	2. -----	2. -----
3.	Kuteans sought permission to destroy Temple, from Alexander.	3. -----	3. -----	3. -----
4.	He gave permission.	4. -----	4. -----	4. -----
5.	Simeon the Just wore priestly garments	5. -----	5. -----	5. -----
6.	and arranged processions.	6. -----	6. -----	6. -----
7.	When morning star arose, approached Alexander.	7. -----	7. -----	7. -----
8.	Who are these? Jews who rebelled against you.	8. -----	8. -----	8. -----

9. At Antipatris sun came out and the processions met.	9. -----	9. -----	9. -----
10. Alexander rose before Simeon, saying if he saw him before battle, he would win.	10. ----- Kuteans asked, Do you rise before a Jew? " " "	10. A. would say, Blessed is God of Simeon the Just. Cour- tiers: Do you rise? A.: See face	10. [As in Pes. de R. Kahana.]
11. Why have you come?	11. -----	11. -----	11. -----
12. You want to destroy the Temple where they pray for you and your kingdom.	12. -----	12. -----	12. -----
13. Gave Kuteans over to Jews, who mutilated them and destroyed Mt. Gerizim.	13 -----	13. -----	13. -----

Clearly, no. 10, which interrupts the narrative of b. Yoma 69a, circulated separately. It was erroneously placed in the Babylonian beraita, presumably because it supplied additional information on Alexander's encounter with Simeon the Just. But it did not explain his favor to the Jews, for immediately thereafter Alexander asks them (no. 11) why the Jews have come, and only after they explain their case in terms favorable to the king does he grant their request, and, more than the request, also the right to take vengeance against the Samaritans.

If the materials in no. 10 circulated by themselves, however, then they may antedate the beraita, for they fit in too well to suggest later contamination. They presumably were shaped before ca. 250 A.D., but appeared only in the late midrashic compilations. This is one instance in which the unredacted form of a story may have independently circulated early, only to be written down long afterward. On the other hand, it is possible that the beraita as we have it was the only redaction of the pericope about Alexander's respect for Simeon, in which case the later midrashic compilers took only a part of it, without the slightest reference to the context in which it had originally appeared. Lev. R. presupposes the connection by including Kuteans. The Pesiqtas improve matters by substituting courtiers -- leaving no problem as to the identity of the questioners.

c. Heavenly echo

Tos. Sot. 13:7 Part A	B. Sot. 33a	Y. Sot. 9:13
1. Simeon the Just heard	1. Further story is told (SWB MSH B) of Simeon the Just that he heard an echo from the house of the Holy of Holies, which was saying	1. The story is told that Simeon the Just heard an echo from the house of the Holy of Holies and said
2. The decree is annulled (BTYLT 'YBYDT)	2. " " "	2. -----
3. which the enemy (SN'H) said (DY'MR)	3. " " "	3. -----
4. to bring (LHYTYH) to the temple	4. " " " to bring (L'YYT'H)	4. -----
5. and QSGLGS has been slain [in Hebrew]	5. " " " GSQLGS	5. GYYS GWLYQS has been slain [in Hebrew]
6. and his decrees are annulled [in Hebrew]	6. " " "	6. and his decrees are annulled [in Hebrew]
7. and he heard them in the Aramaic language	7. [= 9]	7. -----
8. -----	8. and they wrote down the hour and it tallied	8. -----
9. -----	9. And it spoke in the Aramaic language	9. -----

* * * * *

The pericope of Simeon-stories in Tos. Sot. 13:7 splits into two separate traditions. The first tradition is represented here. The second occurs in the next synopsis (p. 41). For y. Sot. 9:13, the point of the story is that Simeon heard a heavenly echo. This version therefore excludes the Aramaic translation of the decrees (nos. 2, 3, and 4), for use of Aramaic is no issue. In other respects y. Sot. does not differ from Tos. nos. 5 and 6. The superscription is simply the story is told concerning, with no reference to a Tannaite tradent. For the Babylonian Talmud and Tosefta, on the other hand, the point of the story is that the heavenly voice spoke in Aramaic. Therefore nos. 2, 3, and 4 are in Aramaic,

but these are in substance then summarized in Hebrew in nos. 5 and 6. No. 6 actually
translates no. 2!

The relationship of the first element in the three versions is fairly clear. The
original was simply Tos. Sot. no 1. This is augmented for editorial purposes with further
in the Babylonian Talmudic account. Both the Babylonian and Palestinian Talmuds include
story is told and supply the information on where the voice came from. From that point
forward Tos. Sot. and b. Sot. are pretty much identical, except for the improvement of
the representation of the verb to bring, and the revision of the spelling of the name of the
enemy. The addition of no. 8 in b. Sot. is clearly a contamination from the foregoing
account, about Yohanan the High Priest (noted above). The passage is quite meaningless
here. No. 7 in Tos. is out of place, for the point of the Tos. stories is not that the echo
spoke in Aramaic. That is the point in b. Sot. 33a. It is a probable contamination.

The several traditions therefore serve quite separate purposes. The point is either
that Simeon heard as echo, or that angels speak Aramaic, but it cannot be both. The
simplest and purest version of the former is y. Sot. Tos. Sot. and b. Sot. have then been
contaminated by the inclusion of both tendencies, resulting in the egregious repetition of
no. 2 in no. 6. If the point were that angels spoke Aramaic, the pertinent elements ought
to have been Tos. Sot. nos. 1-4 and 7, or b. Sot. nos. 1-4 and 9. In neither does no. 8 fit at
all.

No. 1 of the Palestinian Talmudic version comes earlier than no. 1 of the Babylonian. But the relationship of the rest of the elements to one another is unclear to me.
Certainly without Tos. Sot. we should have concluded that b. Sot. came after the version
in the Palestinian Talmud. It would represent a thoroughgoing revision to serve the
purpose of the argument for which it is cited in the Babylonian context. Hence the story
would have been revised later on in Babylonia. But this supposition is impossible, since
the Babylonian version is, except for no. 8, pretty much the same as the one in the
Tosefta; indeed, it is almost certainly based upon it. Hence we have to postulate two
quite separate versions of the pericope: Tos. + b. Sot., or Tos. + y. Sot. The two may be
based upon a common, simple story, of which nos. 5 and 6 in the Palestinian Talmudic
version are an accurate reminiscence. If this is so, then y. Sot. is the earliest of the three
versions, followed by Tosefta, then the Babylonian based upon the Tosefta -- a strange
anomaly.

As to the identification of the enemy referred to in no. 5 of all three accounts, we
have no idea what name is here rendered into Hebrew characters. I see no profit in
attempting to read Gaius Caligula into any of the consonantal representations before us.

d. Miracles

Tos. Sot. 13:7b	Y. Yoma 6:3	B. Yoma 39a-b
1. -----	1. All the days that Simeon the Just was alive, it [the goat] would not reach half-	1. TNW RBNN: In the forty years that Simeon the Just served -- [omits goat-miracle]

			way down the mountain before it was turned into bits. When Simeon the Just died, it would flee to the wilderness, and the Saracens would eat it.		
2.	-----	2.	All the days that Simeon the Just was alive, the lot of the Name would come up in the right [hand]. When Simeon the Just died, sometimes it would come up in the right, sometimes in the left.	2.	" " " [Omits All-alive]
2*.	-----	[2*. see 7*]		2*.	The red strap would turn white. Henceforward, sometimes it would turn white, sometimes it would not turn white. [See y. Yoma 7* below]
3.	All the time that Simeon the Just was alive	3.	days " " "	3.	[Omits all-alive]
4.	The Western lamp was continual (TDYR)	4.	would burn (DLQ)	4.	burn [= y. Yoma]
5.	When he died	5.	" " "	5.	Henceforward
6.	they went and it had gone out	6.	-----	6.	-----
7.	Afterward, sometimes it went out, sometimes it burned	7.	" " "	7.	" " "
7*.	-----	7*.	All the days that Simeon the Just was alive, the red strap would turn white. When Simeon the Just died, sometimes it would turn white,	[7*. = 2* above]	

			8.	All the days etc., the _fire_ of the wood-offering would flame up	8.

sometimes it would turn red.

8. And the fire of the wood-offering was continual

8. All the days etc., the _fire_ of the wood-offering would flame up

8. [Omits <u>all-alive</u>] fire of wood-offering was <u>strong,</u> and the priests <u>did not have to bring wood to the fire except for the two logs to carry out the commandment of the wood.</u>

9. Once they had arranged it in the morning, it was strong (HYTH MTGBRT) all day long

9. Once they <u>had placed two logs</u> in the morning " " "

9. -----

10. and they would offer on it continual offerings and supplementary offerings and their drink-offerings

10. -----

10. -----

11. and they only added to it two logs of the evening offering

11. -----

11. -----

12. Lev. 6:5

12. they added nothing all day long [omits Lev 6:5]

12. -----

13. When Simeon the Just died

13. " " "

13. -----

14. the strength (KH) of the fire-offering diminished (TSS)

14. " " "

14. Henceforward, sometimes it was strong and sometimes it was not strong

15. and they did not refrain from adding wood all day long

15. " " "

15. " " "

16. And there was a blessing on the two loaves of bread and the show-bread.

16. blessing <u>sent</u> upon " " "

16. blessing <u>was sent on the omer and</u> " " "

17. The two loaves of bread were divided at the Gathering (SRT) and the showbread at the festival (RGL) for all the watches.

17. -----

17. -----

18. Some ate and were sated, and some ate and left over

18. Each one would get an olive's bulk and " " "

18. Each priest to whom as much as an olive's came -- some ate " " "

19. and only as much as an olive's bulk came to each one.

19. [See above; order is reversed]

19. [See above, order is reversed.]

20. When Simeon the Just died the blessing departed ...

20. " " "

20. A curse was sent on the omer etc.

21. -----

21. -----

21. [Predicted own death]

* * * * *

B. Yoma 39b

1. TNW RBNN

2. In that year in which Simeon the Just died

B. Men. 109b

1. DTNY'

2. " " "

Y. Yoma 5:2

1. -----

2. Forty years Simeon the Just served Israel in the high priesthood. In the last year, he said to them, In this year I am going to die.

3. he said to them that in this year he would die

3. " " "

3. [As above]

4. They said to him, Whence do you know?

4. " " "

4. " " "

5. He said to them, Every Day of Atonement an old man would meet me, dressed in white and cloaked in white.

5. " " "

5. He said to them, Every

6.	He would enter with me and leave with me.	6.	" " "	6.	" " "
7.	Today an old man met me dressed in black and cloaked in black. He went in with me but he did not leave with me.	7.	" " "	7.	This year he entered with me but did not leave with me. [Omits black clothes]
8.	After the festival he fell ill for seven days and he died.	8.	" " "	8.	-----
9.	His brethren the priests held back from blessing with the [Ineffable] name.	9.	" " "	9.	-----
10.	-----	10.	When he was dying, he said to them, My son Onias etc. [The rest of the story appears only here.]	10.	-----
[11. -----]		[11. -----]		[11. Colloquy of R. Abbahu: Man was the Holy One.]	

The changes in the supernatural setting of the cult and the prediction by Simeon that he would die are as follows:

Tos. Sot. 13:7b		Y. Yoma 6:9		B. Yoma 39a-b		Men. 109b		Y. Yoma 5:2	
1.	Western lamp	1.	Goat	1.	Lot	1.	Predicted death	1.	Prayed too long
2.	Fire of wood-offering	2.	Lot	2.	Red strap	2.	Ineffable Name	2.	Predicted death
3.	Blessing of loaves	3.	Western lamp	3.	Western lamp				
		4.	Red strap	4.	Fire of wood-offering				

5.	Fire of wood-offering	5.	Blessing of loaves
6.	Blessing of loaves	6.	Predicted death
		7.	Ineffable Name

If we could reconstruct a single, unitary source that underlay the several pericopae, it logically would look something like this:

	1.	Prayed too long
	2.	Predicted death and died
Day of Atonement	3.	Priests stop saying Ineffable Name
	4.	After he died: Goat
	5.	Lot
	6.	Red Strap
	7.	Western lamp
Daily Cult	8.	Fire of wood-offering
	9.	Blessing of loaves

Nos. 1-6 all pertain to the Day of Atonement. Nos. 7-9 stand by themselves as a comparable, but separate list of supernatural changes. Strikingly, Tos. Sot. does preserve nos. 7-9 as a separate pericope. Similarly, b. Yoma 39a-b, nos. 6-7, probably circulated separately, as seen in the identical version in b. Men. 109b. There the pericope serves to introduce the long singleton about the succession to Simeon. Palestinian Talmud Yoma 5:2 similarly supplies the Yom Kippur pericope, but without the miracles in connection with the cult of that day. That leaves the lists in y. Yoma 6:3 and b. Yoma 39a-b, in which the Yom Kippur miracles are presented together with those of Tos. Sot.; but b. Yoma keeps the Yom Kippur materials separate from the other miracles, while y. Yoma inserts no. 3, Western lamp, into the midst of the others. We may therefore take it for granted that Tos. Sot. does constitute a single, separate pericope. The stories about the prediction of Simeon's death probably circulated separately as well, therefore serving diverse editorial purposes later on. To these were attached the detail about the Ineffable Name or the prayer that went on too long; neither was integral to the prediction-story, but both found a satisfactory place. The miracles connected with the Day of Atonement service likewise may have circulated by themselves, but in the form before us they have already been contaminated by the list of Tos. Sot.

As to the relationships among the several components of the pericopae, we find that the Babylonian beraita imposed its own conventional language, as would be expected. Normally, this meant choosing words common in Babylonian rabbinical Hebrew and rendering vague details more precise and pointed, e.g. all the days of y. Yoma becomes in the forty years. But the substance of the several miracles varies very little between the Palestinian and Babylonian versions. The important differences are between both and Tosefta. Thus Tos. Sot. 13:7b, nos. 6, 9, 10, 11, and 17 have no close equivalent, or no equivalent at all, in either Talmudic version. The Babylonian version, to be sure, transforms the participle of y. Yoma 6:3 no. 16 into a verb, adds omer (no. 20), and makes a few other, minor alterations. But in the main Tos. presents a striking contrast to the two Talmuds' versions, and these by and large closely resemble one another.

The beraita in b. Yoma 39b is unchanged in b. Men. 109b. I imagine the editor of b. Men. 109b took it from existing materials to serve as an introduction to the story of real interest to him, about the Temple of Onias. Without the foregoing materials (nos. 1-9) the story told by R. Meir could have stood by itself. The death-story in b. Yoma 39b and y. Yoma 5:2 presents some contrasts. The Palestinian Talmudic version makes explicit the forty years, but that detail had already occurred in b. Yoma 39a-b. Perhaps the editor of the beraita saw no reason to repeat the information. Since the y. Yoma pericope stands by itself, it was natural to include the more concrete detail. Hence we cannot in this instance suppose the Palestinian version to have been more detailed or concrete than the Babylonian one. The indirect discourse of the Babylonian beraita becomes direct discourse (or vice versa) in no 2. The detail about the old man dressed in white is omitted in no. 7 of the Palestinian version. It seems to me a striking omission, and the likelihood is that the editor of the Babylonian beraita supplied it to complete the symmetry of the story. He likewise invented nos. 8 and 9; no. 8 is absolutely necessary to complete the tale -- that is, Simeon actually did die. No. 9 is not essential. In any event, the Babylonian beraita probably comes after the Palestinian version of the same story and likely depends upon it. The augmentations are not derived from a separate oral or written tradition circulating by itself, but all were provoked by literary and artistic considerations. None presents a detail of independent, historical interest.

CHAPTER THREE
ANTIGONOS OF SOKHO
YOSE B. YOEZER AND YOSE B. YOHANAN

A. Yose b. Yoezer and Yose b. Yohanan

1. Reproach against Grapeclusters

Tos. B.Q. 8:13	Y. Sot. 9:10	B. Tem. 15b-16a
		1.* And Rav Judah said in the name of Samuel, All the grapeclusters " " " from the days of Moses until Yosef b. Yoezer died would learn Torah like Moses our rabbi. Thenceforward, they did not learn Torah like Moses our rabbi.
1. All the grape-clusters that arose from Israel from when Moses died until Yosef b. Yoezer of Seredah and Yosef b. Yohanan of Jerusalem	1. TNY: Pairs (ZWGWT) " " "	1. TNY: All the grapeclusters that arose for Israel from the days of Moses until Yose b. Yoezer died
2. It is not possible to place reproach against them.	2. It is possible	2. There was not in them any reproach
3. And until arose Judah b. Baba	3. " " " [omits: and]	3. -----
4. It is possible to place against them reproach	4. It is not possible	4. Thenceforward, there was in them reproach

The Tos. has been much garbled in transmission to the Babylonian beraita, no less so to the Palestinian version. As to the latter, we observe that the sense of the tradition has been reversed. The beraita begins with the teaching in Samuel's name about study of Torah, followed by TNY as in 1* above. It seems to represent at best a paraphrase of Tos. Yose b. Yohanan has been dropped in both parts of the Babylonian Talmudic version; Judah b. Baba (no. 3) is likewise omitted here, but is referred to in the immediately following Talmudic discussion. This proves that the beraita originally contained no reference to him, for if it had, the subsequent discussion, aimed at showing Judah is referred to, would have been superfluous. The Babylonian beraita thus has drawn the sting from the Judah b. Baba-tradition, by leaving the impression that while the end of the grapeclusters concluded old-time virtue, no particular sage later on can be credited with reverting to that former glory. Without the praise of Judah b. Baba as the restorer of ancient merit, the beraita has been deprived of its former contemporary relevance. It stands merely as an untendentious supplement to the grapecluster-Mishnah.

I imagine the beraita was shaped after the version in Tos. B.Q., indeed after Judah, the language of whose citation of Samuel suggests that the original formulation of Tos. B.Q. was unknown. Had it been known to Judah (Samuel), he would have directly referred to it and would not have offered his own formulation, involving study of Torah, of the change in the history of the grapecluster.

Alternatively, Samuel Judah did know Tos. B.Q., but, because of its political aspect (Judah b. Baba), preferred to formulate it in other, quite original, but neutral terms. But the baraita in any event accomplished the same end. It may, to be sure, have been formulated after the Judah b. Baba-version and circulated independently thereafter. The omission of Yose/Yosef b. Yohanan later on could not have been consequential. He was merely a name on a list. No one had ties to him or direct access to traditions originally deriving from him.

2. Uncleanness of Land of Peoples and Glassware

B. Shab. 14b	Y. Shab. 1:4	Y. Pes. 1:6	Y. Ket. 8:11
1. DTNY	1. Did not R. Zeira b. Abuna in R. Jeremiah's name say	1. Did not R. Zeira R. Abuna " "	Did not " "
2. Yose + Yose	2. Yosef + Yosef	2. Yose + Yose	2. Yose + Yose
3. decreed uncleanness	3. " " "	3. " " "	3. " " "
4. on the land of the peoples	4. " " "	4. " " "	4. " " "

5. and on glassware	5. " " "	5. " " "	5. " " "
5.* -----	5.* R. Yonah said, Judah b. Tabbai	5.* " " "	5.* R. Yose said, Judah b. Tabbi R. Yonah said, Judah b. Tabbi and Simeon b. Shetah decreed...
6. Simeon b. Shetah ordained (TQN)	6. And Simeon b. Shetah decreed	6. [= y. Shab.]	6. [As above]
7. marriage-settlement for a wife	7. -----	7. -----	7. -----
8. and decreed uncleanness on metal utensils	8. " " "	8. " " "	8. " " "
9. Shammai and Hillel decreed	9. Hillel and Shammai " " "	9. Hillel and Shammai " " "	9. Hillel and Shammai " " "
10. uncleanness on the hands	10. " " "	10. cleanness " " "	10. cleanness " " "

What the Babylonian Talmud knows as a beraita allegedly formulated by Tannaim is available to the Palestinian Talmud only in the names of fourth-century Palestinian Amoraim from Babylonia (Jeremiah, Zeira). That is not surprising, as we saw in Chapter One. Apart from the marriage-contract (no. 7), the materials are nearly identical in all important matters. Variations are in such minor details as the names Yose/Yosef. The Palestinian versions are virtually identical with one another. b. Shab.'s S + H is the better order; and uncleanness (no. 10) must be more accurate than cleanness, which makes no sense. But the inclusion of no. 7 is irrelevant to decrees on purity laws -- indeed, the language TQN is substituted, obviously unsatisfactorily, for GZR, otherwise used throughout. Alternatively, the beraita before us has been contaminated by materials from other sources.

B. Yose b. Yoezer Alone

1. Cleanness of Fluids in Temple Slaughter-house

Sifra 8:5	M. Ed. 8:4	B. Pes. 16a	B. Ned. 19a	B. A.Z. 37a
1. Rabbi Eliezer says	1. -----	1. WHTNY: Eleazar	1. [As b. Pes.]	1. DTNN
2. Unclean-ness (TWMH) etc.	2. -----	2. " " "	2. " " "	2. -----
3. You should know that it is so	3. -----	3. [Omits: that]	3. [As b. Pes.]	3. -----
4. for be-hold, Yose b. Seredah testified concerning	4. [Omits: for be-hold; Adds: b. Yoezer] " " "	4. " " "	4. [As b. Pes.]	4. " " "
4.* -----	4.* on ayil-QMSDKY	4.* DKN	4.* [As. b. Pes.]	4.* " " DKN
5. BYMTHBHY	5. and on fluid of the slaughter-house (MSQH BYT MTBHY)	5. MSQYN	5. [As. b. Pes.]	5. MSQH
6. that [they are] pure (DKYNN)	6. that they are pure (DYNWN DKYN)	6. " " " DKN	6. " " "	6. DKN

| 7. ----- | 7. And that one who touches a corpse is impure (WDYQRB BMYT MSTB) | 7. ------ | 7. ----- | 7. [As in Mishnah] LMYT MSB |
| 8. ----- | 8. And they called him Yose the lenient (WQRW LH YWSY SRY) | 8. ----- | 8. ----- | 8. [As in Mishnah] LYH YWSP |

The citation of the Mishnah in b. A.Z. 37a is accurate and reveals only minor variations, none of which changes the meaning. The beraita-versions of b. Pes. and b. Ned are identical. Both differ markedly from the Mishnah in omitting nos. 7 and 8. But the real comparison is between Mishnah and Sifra. Sifra is shorter, leaving out all but the question of fluids (nos. 5-6). The rulings however pertain to uncleanness. I suppose the Mishnah preserves the earliest formulation of the saying, that is, the full list in Aramaic. Then Sifra presents merely part of it, for R. Eliezer's purposes. To be sure, the brief citation (nos. 5-6) could have been an independent tradition, circulating quite separately from the list of three Yose-rulings supplied by M. Ed. In any event the entire list in M. Ed. now forms a unified pericope. Two of the three rulings are lenient and are so characterized at the end (no. 8).

CHAPTER FOUR
JOSHUA B. PERAHIAH AND NITTAI THE ARBELITE
JUDAH B. TABBAI AND SIMEON B. SHETAH

A. Judah b. Tabbai and Simeon b. Shetah
1. Man Illegally Put to Death and Anomaly of Law against Circumstantial Evidence

Mekh. Kaspa III 31-41		Tos. Sanh. 6:6 = Mid. Tan. ed. Hoffmann, p. 112		Tos. Sanh. 8:3
1.	Once (KBR) S. killed (HRG) a false witness	1.	Judah said -----	1. -----
2.	Judah b. Tabbai said to him	2.	-----	2. -----
3.	May I [not] see consolation if you have not shed innocent blood [= Tos. 7*]	3.	May I " " if I have not slain a perjurer to uproot from the Boethusians who say the accused must be put to death [before the perjurer is slain] (Mid. Tan. = Sadducees)	3. -----
4.	and the Torah said	4.	-----	4. -----
5.	Slay at the testimony of witnesses, slay at the testimony of perjurers	5.	-----	5. -----
6.	Just as the witnesses are two	6.	-----	6. -----
7.	so the perjurers are two	7.	-----	7. -----

7.* -----

7.* Simeon said to him, May I [etc.] if you have not shed innocent blood

7.* -----

7** -----

7** = Mekh. 6, 7

7** -----

8. and once (WKBR)

8. -----

8. Simeon said, May I [etc.] if I did not see one running after his fellow with a sword in his hand. He entered before him into a ruin, and ran after him.

9. Judah b. Tabbai entered a ruin.

9. -----

9. I entered after him.

10. and found there a slain man still writhing (MPRPR)

10. -----

10. and found him slain

11. and the sword dripping blood (MNTP DM)

11. -----

11. and the sword in the hand of the murderer " "

12. from the hand of the slayer

12. -----

12. [see above]

13. Judah b. Tabbai said to him, May [evil] come upon me

13. -----

13. I said to him, Wicked one -- " " "

14. if not you or I have slain him

14. -----

14. " " "

15. But what should I do

15. -----

15. " " " for your case is not given into my hand

16. for lo, the Torah said, At the testimony of two witnesses (Deut. 19:15)

16. -----

16. " " "

17. But he who knows and the master of thoughts (HYWD WBL HMHSBWT)	17. -----	17. [Omits: <u>master of</u>]
18. he will exact punishment of that man	18. -----	18. " " "
19. He had hardly come out when a serpent bit him and he died.	19. -----	19. He did not <u>move</u> from there " " "
20. -----	20. At that moment Judah took on himself not to teach law except according to Simeon. [Mid. Tan. copies b. Mak. 5b, no. 20.]	20. -----

The Tosefta has split the single but composite pericope of Mekh. Kaspa into its two components; the first, about killing a perjurer, is separated from the story about circumstantial evidence. In both instances Judah is replaced as the hero by Simeon. Further, the Tos.'s Simeon now tells Judah he has shed innocent blood; the Mekhilta's Judah says the same to Simeon. The Tos.'s Judah explains his action: to inflict exemplary punishment. Of this Mekh. knows nothing. Tos. no. 3 seems to depend on Mekh. no. 1. The Tos.'s version of the unpunishable murder is similar to the Mekhilta's and in most respect depends upon it, e.g. in the correction of <u>master of</u> (no. 17), which is redundant, and in strengthening the conclusion (no. 19) by killing the man in the very presence of the rabbi. Likewise no. 13 is intensified by the expletive <u>wicked</u>. The whole account is now given in the first person, as the narrative of Simeon himself. Both Toseftan versions are developments of the Mekhilta's composite pericope. But the developments are not merely of detail, which would permit us to impute dependency. Rather, the names of the masters are consistently reversed, and this suggests deliberate doctoring, not merely the augmentation of one detail or another. The further versions all depend in general upon the Toseftan one, as we shall now see. Mekhilta stands mostly apart from the later developments of the pericope. For the next stage in the comparison, we shall give y. Sanh. 4:9, to which the other versions will be compared.

y. Sanh. 4:9 = Mid. Tan. ed. Hoffmann, p. 101	y. Sanh. 6:3	b. Mak. 5b
1. Simeon said, May I see consolation	1. -----	1. -----

2.	If I did not see one pursuing another	2.	-----	2.	-----
3.	He entered [Mid. Tan.: ran] a ruin	3.	-----	3.	-----
4.	I entered after him	4.	-----	4.	-----
5.	and found him slain	5.	-----	5.	-----
6.	and this one going out	6.	-----	6.	-----
7.	and the sword was dripping blood	7.	-----	7.	-----
8.	I said to him	8.	-----	8.	-----
9.	May I see consolation	9.	-----	9.	-----
10.	that this one slew him	10.	-----	10.	-----
11.	but what shall I do	11.	-----	11.	-----
12.	for your blood is not given into my hands	12.	-----	12.	-----
13.	but the one who knows thoughts will exact punishment from that man	13.	-----	13.	-----
14.	He did not even leave there [HSPYQ LST]	14.	-----	14.	-----
15.	before a serpent bit him and he died.	15.	-----	15.	-----

16. -----	16. Judah b. Tabbai said, May I see consolation if I did not slay a false witness. For they would say, Until he is slain [the false witness is not punished], as it is said (Ex. 21:23), <u>Soul for soul</u>	16. TNY " " " " " " to remove from the <u>heart of the Sadducees</u> who would <u>say</u> " " "
17. -----	17. Simeon b. Shetah said to him, May I see consolation	17. " " "
18. -----	18. if it is not regarded to you as if you shed innocent blood.	18. <u>if you did not shed</u> " " " for the sages said, <u>no</u> <u>punishment until the</u> <u>accused perjurers are</u> <u>both found guilty</u> [+ <u>flagellation</u> and <u>fines,</u> in same formula]
19. -----	19. At that time he took upon himself not to teach except from the mouth of Simeon b. Shetah	19. " " " except <u>in the</u> <u>presence</u> " " "
20. -----	20. -----	20. <u>And all the rest of</u> <u>Judah's life he</u> <u>prostrated himself on</u> <u>the grave of that</u> <u>witness, and his voice</u> <u>was heard, and people</u> <u>thought it was the voice</u> <u>of the slain man.</u> He <u>said, It is my voice.</u> <u>You</u> ill <u>know it tomorrow</u> <u>when he dies.</u>

* * * * *

B. Sanh.	B. Shav. 34a	B. Hag. 16b
1. TNY " " "	1. " " "	1. -----
2. " " " another into a ruin	2. " " " [as b. Sanh.]	2. -----
3. I ran after him	3. " " "	3. -----
4. -----	4. -----	4. -----
5. I saw him with a sword in his hand	5. I found him " " "	5. -----
6. -----	6. -----	6. -----
7. and his blood was dripping and the slain man was writhing	7. " " " [as b. Sanh.]	7. -----
8. " " "	8. " " "	8. -----
9. -----	9. -----	9. -----
10. Wicked! Who killed this man? You or me	10. " " "	10. -----
11. " " "	11. " " "	11. -----
12. " " " for lo, the Torah has said Deut. 17	12. " " "	12. -----
13. " " " from that man who slew his fellow	13. The Omnipresent will " " " from you [omits who-fellow]	13. -----
14. They said he did not move from there before a snake came and bit him and he died	14. " they did not move before a snake bit him [omits came and]	14. -----
15. [As above]	15. [As above]	15. -----

16. -----	16. -----	16. TNW RBNN
17. -----	17. -----	17. [As b. Mak. 5b]
18. -----	18. -----	18. [As b. Mak. 5b]
19. -----	19. -----	19. [As b. Mak. 5b]
20. -----	20. -----	20. [As b. Mak. 5b]

The beraita about Judah's exemplary but illegal punishment of the false witness, b. Mak. 5b = b. Hag. 16b, is an improvement on the equivalent version in y. Sanh. 6:3. There they would say is unclear. The Babylonian version supplies the identity of those who held the false opinion, namely the Sadducees. This further depends upon Tos. Sanh. 6:6, but Boethusians is dropped in favor of Sadducees. The exact quotation of the Boethusians/Sadducees varies somewhat. y. Sanh. supplies a proof-text for their opinion, which is absent in Tos. Sanh. and later dropped in b. Mak. = b. Hag. The most striking change occurs in no. 18, where the language if it is not regarded to you as if you shed is changed to the more direct you shed. This is a simplification and an improvement. Tos. knows nothing of Judah's pledge not to teach instruction/law except according to Simeon, which occurs in more dramatic detail -- in the presence of -- in the Babylonian beraita. The Palestinian is intermediate; it does not specify what it was that Judah would not teach. The beraita, in summary, is unquestionably later than, and an improvement upon, y. Sanh., being smoother, dropping irrelevant details (e.g. the proof-text), but supplying important "omissions", e.g. what Judah would not teach, and adding flagellation and fines. In one respect, namely no. 16, to remove etc., the beraita obviously must depend upon Tos. But in all other important aspects, it is a development of y. Sanh. 6:3 -- thus eclectic or a composite, a puzzling result.

The Mekh. version provides the briefest and least satisfactory story, omits the dramatic details of Judah's (Simeon's) report of what he had done, and of Judah's vow not to teach except following Simeon's opinions. No. 20 of the beraita is certainly a dramatic and colorful addition to the whole, known only in the latest version.

The story about the murderer whom the law cannot punish is linked to the foregoing in Mekh. Kaspa, but everywhere else stands separately. In Mekh. Kaspa we again find the simplest and least embellished form. The changes from y. Sanh. 4:9 to b. Sanh. 37b = b. Shav. 34a are not considerable. The scene is somewhat clarified and sharpened. He entered... I entered of y. Sanh. becomes the dramatic confrontation of b. Sanh.: I ran after him and saw him a moment after he did the deed. Then the details (no. 7) are greatly augmented, but again are drawn mainly from Mekh. Kaspa, further from the anomymous accounts, not summarized here, which invariably include the gory details. What shall I do of y. Sanh. 4:9 is greatly expanded by reference to the proof-text, but here this is artfully introduced in the context of the exchange between the sage and the murderer. Then, in no. 14 of b. Sanh., the narrator takes over for the unclear he did not leave, so we are now told who has provided the details of the denouement.

As we observed above, the two stories are distinct and circulated by themselves. Only the Judah b. Tabbai-version was kept together. The Simeon-ones were allowed to develop separately. The beraitot in both cases provide additional information, but we have not reason to suppose they contain material drawn from other, independent traditions. In each instance, on the basis of the earlier versions we can readily account for the alterations. Only no. 20 is entirely independent of the foregoing, but it is certainly a dramatic embellishment, nothing more; it is the sort of addition that editors of beraitot loved to make.

Now, assuming the Mekhilta is the earliest version of the pericopae, we note that the later accounts are in general dependent upon, or at least related to, it in all important details except for the identification of the hero. The whole can be said to be a living tradition, in that details found later on normally derive from earlier accounts and can be readily traced from one version to the next. But what lies before Mekh. Kaspa? I find it difficult to imagine that the literary relationships we have observed do not signify the dependence, upon the Mekhilta, of the accounts in which Simeon is the hero. The Mekhilta of R. Ishmael-version is what Meir would have supplied; all the others in general follow opinion of Judah b. Ilai, making Simeon Nasi. All elements of the Simeon-materials thus are revisions of the foregoing, including the important fact that Simeon is the hero, Judah the judge who erred. In that case, the correct tradition must be the one which places Judah b. Tabbai superior to Simeon b. Shetah. The others testify to the ability of Judah b. Ilai and those who shared his view not only to develop the older tradition, but also completely to revise its historical and biographical facts. The relative importance of Simeon and Judah seems to have constituted an important issue for the late second century Tannaitic schools.

2. Nasi -- Head of Court

Tos. Hag. 2:8	Y. Hag. 2:2a	Y. Sanh. 6:6a
1. There were five pairs.	1. -----	1. -----
2. Three of the first pairs who said not to lay on hands	2. -----	2. -----
3. and two of the last who said to lay on hands	3. -----	3. -----
4. were Nasis,	4. -----	4. -----

5. and the second were heads of court, according to R. Meir	5. -----	5. -----
6. R. Judah says, Simeon b. Shetah was <u>Nasi</u>, Judah b. Tabbai head of the court	6. [As in 6*]	6. [As in 6*]
6.* -----	6.* We have learned (NN TNYNN): Judah b. Tabbai was <u>Nasi</u>, Simeon b. Shetah was head of the court.	6.* Some Tannaim teach (YT TNYY TNY) Judah b. Tabbai was <u>Nasi</u>, and some Tannaim teach Simeon b. Shetah was <u>Nasi</u>.
7. -----	7. Some teach it in reverse. [The story of Judah in Alexandria and Simeon in Ashqelon follows.]	7. -----

The Tos. version thus has not been reproduced, merely cited, in the Palestinian Amoraic discussion. But y. Hag. rephrases the whole in explicit form: Judah was <u>Nasi</u>, Simeon was head of the court. In y. Sanh. two separate attributions to Tannaim simply assign the position of <u>Nasi</u> to each of the authorities. In any event the language of Tos. has been abandoned, while Tannaitic authority is claimed for its content.

3. Judah b. Tabbai in Alexandria

<u>Y. Hag. 2:2b</u>   <u>Y. Sanh. 6:6b</u>

1. The men of Jerusalem wanted to appoint Judah b. T. as <u>nasi</u> in Jerusalem. He fled to Alexandria.	1. -----
2. The men of Jerusalem would write	2. " " "
3. From Jerusalem the great, to Alexandria the small	3. " " "

4. How long will my betrothed dwell with you, and I set etc.	4. How long will my husband dwell in your midst " " " in my house
5. He departed, coming in a boat. He said, you remember etc.	5. [Omits the affair with the student.]

The version in y. Sanh. omits the introductory materials and knows nothing of the incident with the student at all. The augmentations in no. 4 suggest a somewhat later version, and my guess is that y. Sanh. depends upon, but abbreviates, y. Hag. The same pattern of summary and abbreviation of y. Hag. by y. Sanh. recurs in the Simeon-story.

4. The Decree on the Uncleanness of Metal Utensils

B. Shab. 14b	Y. Shab. 1:4	Y. Pes. 1:6	Y. Ket. 8:11
1. DTNY	1. R. Zeira b. Abuna in the name of R. Jeremiah	1. [As y. Shab.] R. Abuna	1. [As y. Pes.]
2. Yose b. Yoezer and Yose b. Yohanan decreed uncleanness on the land of the peoples and glassware.	2. " " "	2. " " "	2. " " "
3. Simeon b. Shetah ordained (TQN) the marriage contract for the woman	3. R. Yonah said, Judah b. Tabbai. R. Yose said, Judah b. Tabbai and Simeon b. Shetah decreed uncleanness on metalware [Omits marriage-contract]	3. R. Judah said, Judah b. T. and and Simeon b. S. [As. y. Shab.]	3. R. Yosi said Judah b. T.R. Yonah said, Judah b. T. and Simeon b. S. decreed uncleanness on metalware [Omits marriage-contract]

4. and decreed (GZR) uncleanness on metalware	4. [See no. 3]	4. [See no. 3]	4. [See no. 3]
5. Shammai and Hillel decreed uncleanness on the hands	5. " " concerning the cleanness of the hands	5. [As y. Shab.]	5. [As y. Shab.]

Since y. Ket. 8:11 contains the list of Simeon's decrees, we shall add the synopsis of that list here:

Tos. Ket. 12:1	B. Ket. 82b	Y. Ket. 8:11
1. At first... Simeon b. S. ordained that her marriage-contract should be with her husband, and he should write to her, All the property which I have is liable and pledged for this, your marriage-contract	1. Rab Judah... Simeon b. S. ordained all his property is liable for her marriage-contract. TNY NMY HKY: ...until Simeon b. S. ordained that he should write to her, All my property is liable for her marriage-contract	1. Simeon b. Shetah decreed three things
2. -----	2. -----	2. That a man may do business with his wife's marriage-contract
3. -----	3. -----	3. That children should go to school
4. -----	4. -----	4. and he ordained (TQN) uncleanness on glassware

All the references to the marriage-contract pertain to details. None holds Simeon b. Shetah invented the marriage-contract. The reference in b. Shab. no. 4 appears in y. Ket. 8:11 no. 4, now an ordinance. The version in b. Shab. no. 4 is unrelated to more detailed accounts of the matter. The marriage-contract materials are not closely related. Tos. Ket. has certainly produced b. Ket., but y. Ket. (like b. Shab. no. 3) stands pretty much by itself. Perhaps the intent of the ordinance is what y. Ket. no. 2 maintains, but that is not what is specified.

As to the decree on the uncleanness of metal utensils, all the traditions are identical in language, except y. Ket. no. 4, which, like b. Shab. no. 4, omits reference to Judah b. Tabbai. Since the lists of b. Shab. 14b and y. Ket. 8:11 have in common the omission of Judah b. Tabbai and a reference to the marriage-contract (but not the same reference), there may be some correspondence between them. But a list of Simeon's decrees ought not to have omitted the founding of the school-system, and TQN of y. Ket. changes to GZR in b. Shab. Hence the lists are not closely related. Moreover, the intent of y. Ket. 8:11 is to list Simeon's decrees; one might argue Judah b. Tabbai is not deliberately omitted, merely bypassed for stylistic purposes. But the same cannot be said for b. Shab. 14b, which either is defective or represents a purposeful revision of the tradition referred to by the Palestinian Amoraim. I presume the latter were influenced by the juxtaposition of Judah and Simeon in M. Hag. 2:2 and M. Avot (see Chapter Fourteen), but I do not understand why the framer of the Babylonian beraita was not similarly impressed with those lists, if he knew them.

B. Simeon b. Shetah Alone

1. Heavy Rains

Sifra	B. Ta. 23a	Lev. R.
1. M^CSH	1. So we find	1. " " "
2. In the days of Simeon b. S., in the days of SLMSW the queen	2. " " " [Omits: Salome the Queen]	2. " " " (SLMSY) [Adds:] and
3. that the rains would descend from Sabbath night to Sabbath night	3. " " " on eves of Wednesdays and Sabbaths	3. " " "
4. until the wheat was made like kidneys	4. " " "	4. " " "
5. the barley like olive pits	5. " " "	5. " " "
6. and the lentils like gold denars	6. " " "	6. " " "

7. and the sages bound up (SRR) some of them	7. " " " as an example (DWGM)	7. " " "
8. and left them for coming generations	8. " " " [Omits: and left them; coming]	8. " " "
9. to make known how much sin causes,	9. " " "	9. All this why " " "
10. to fulfill that which is said Jer. 5:25	10. As it is said " " "	10. " " "

The differences between Lev. R. and Sifra are negligible. Only all this why betrays the mark of a later hand. The phrase could have been omitted without loss of meaning. It serves to underline the purposive sense of the infinitive, to make known. The Babylonian Talmudic version follows the usual Amoraic form, as it is said, in place of the Tannaitic midrashic to fulfill. Salome is now omitted, certainly an improvement, dropping a redundant detail; her name could have meant little to people out of touch with the stories of King Yannai and Simeon. Wednesdays is added because of the legal context. As an example likewise clarifies the sages' intent, thought it does not augment the meaning. The version in b. Ta. is certainly a development of that in Sifra. Lev. R. is a more exact copy. This is a common phenomenon. Where traditions appearing in early collections recur in very late ones, they are normally copies, showing little evidence of either growth of a living tradition, or response to vivid discussions of the subject-matter of the pericope. Both phenomena by contrast are apparent in b. Ta. Sometimes, to be sure, late compilations supply all sorts of new elements, but these rarely appear to be integral to the earlier version or part of an internal process of augmentation of words or phrases. Rather, they tend to be manufactured of whole cloth.

2. Hung Eighty Women in Ashqelon

Sifre Deut. 221	M. Sanh. 6:4	Y. Sanh. 6:3
1. The man is hung, but not the woman. R. Eliezer says, Even a woman is to be hung.	1. The woman is hung facing backward, the man facing the people, so R. Eliezer. The sages say, The man is hung, but not the woman.	1. -----
2. R. Eliezer said to them, Did not Simeon	2. " " "	2. -----

b. S. hang women in
Ashqelon?

3.	They said to him, He hung eighty women, and one does not judge two on the same day	3.	" " "	3.	-----
4.	But hour required to teach other by that means	4.	-----	4.	-----
5.	-----	5.	-----	5.	Simeon's hands were heated. A conspiracy of scoffers came and said, Come, let us take counsel and testify against his son and kill him. They testified against him and his case was settled that he be killed. As he was going forth to be killed, they said to him, "My lord, we are liars." His father wanted to bring him back. He said to him, "Father, if you want salvation to come at your hand, make me like a threshold."

* * * * *

Y. Hag. 2:2c	Y. Sanh. 6:6c
1. There were two pious men who shared their food and studies.	1. " " "
2. One died and was not properly mourned.	2. " " "

3. When a villager, a tax-collector died, the whole town took time off to mourn him.

3. " " "

4. The pious man began to be troubled and said etc.

4. " " " to cry

5. Do not disgrace the sons of your Lord, for this one did one sin, and the other one did one good deed and it went well for him

5. " " " [minor variations, one sin and went in it, one good deed and went in it]

6. [Specifies the sin; then second dream: pious man saw fellow in heaven, tax-collector suffering, Because she fasted etc.]

6. [Specifies sin; omits: sin of Miriam.]
    and Miriam etc. Why is this so?

7. How long thus?

7. " " "

8. Until Simeon takes it from her ear and puts in it his?

8. " " "

9. Why? Because he said, If I am made Nasi I shall kill witches, and lo, he had been made Nasi and has not killed witches. There are eighty in a cave in Ashqelon. Go and tell him.

9. What is his lapse? He vowed and said " " "

10. I am afraid, for he is Nasi and will not believe me. If he believes you, well and good, and if not, this is your sign [re eye].

10. " " " (Minor variations)

11. Simeon believed him

11. " " "

12. Took eighty young men etc.

12. [From here to end, the account is abbreviated and simplified.]

13. This is what we learned, The story is told of Simeon b. Shetah that he hung women in Ashqelon. They

13. This is what we learned, Eighty women did Simeon b. S. hang in Ashqelon and one does not judge two

said he hung eighty women; while | in one day, but the hour required

one does not judge two on the same | it.

day, the hour required it.

The tradition on the hanging of (eighty) women (witches) in Ashqelon comes in two forms. The earliest is a reference merely to hanging women. Nothing more is told. This tradition is virtually ignored in y. Hag. and y. Sanh., which produce the elaborate account about the witches and how they were outwitted by Simeon's superior knowledge of magic and of the libido of witches. A still further detail records the vengeance of the people of Ashqelon. It seems to me Sifre must be regarded as earliest, and the Palestinian Amoraic versions as quite separate, but much later assemblies of traditions. According to the former, Simeon did put to death a large number of women, but we do not know why. The elaborate accounts of y. Sanh. and y. Hag. supply the reason and much more. Of the two, y. Hag. is the more detailed, while y. Sanh. seems to be an abbreviation and a summary. But neither is likely to date before Amoraic times. The Babylonian Talmud contains no equivalent materials, and we may perhaps assign the magical accounts to third- or fourth-century Palestinian schools.

3. Rebuked Honi

M. Ta. 3:8	Y. M.Q. 3:1	Y. Ta. 3:10
1. ...Simeon b. S. sent to him	1. [All omitted to here.] " " " He said to him	1. [Mishnah ends with Prov. 23:25. Then] If a decree were decreed as in the days of Elijah, would you not be found bringing the public to profanation of the name [etc. as in y. M.Q. no. 2.]
2. Were you not Honi	2. You ought to be excommunicated. For if a decree were decreed as in the days of Elijah, would you not be found bringing the public to profanation of the name, for all who bring the public to profanation of the name require excommunication.	2. [as y. M.Q.]

3. I should decree   3.   -----   3.   -----
excommunication upon
you

4. But what should I do
to you

5. For you come   5.   -----   5.   -----
petulantly (HTY) before
the Omnipresent

6. and he does your will   6.   -----   6.   -----
for you

7. like a son who comes   7.   -----   7.   -----
petulantly against his
father

8. and he does his will   8.   -----   8.   -----

9. and concerning you   9.   -----   9.   -----
Scripture says Prov.
23:25

* * * * *

B. Ber. 19a

1. DTNN [Omits story until Simeon
sent to him] " " " You require to
be excommunicated

2. " " "

3. " " "

4. " " "

5. " " "

B. Ta. 23a

1. [Foregoing story much developed.
Then as in M. Ta.] " " "

2. For if the years were like the years of
Elijah, for the keys of rain were in the
hand of Elijah, would not the name of
heaven be found profaned by your hand.

3. [As above]

4. " " "

5. " " "

6. " " "	6. " " "
7. " " "	7. " " "
8. " " "	8. " " " [Adds:] <u>and he says to him, Father,</u> <u>take me to wash me in warm water, pour</u> <u>cold water over me, give me nuts,</u> <u>almonds, and pomegranates and he gives</u> <u>him</u>
9. " " "	9. " " "

The Palestinian Amoraic versions introduce the theme of Elijah, but drop the rest of the colloquy of Simeon. The Babylonian <u>beraita</u> (b. Ber. 19a) borrows a single phrase, <u>You</u> <u>require</u>. The extended version in b. Ta. 3a not only adopts the whole of the Palestinian version, but then inserts the remainder of the Mishnah passage, and finally supplies a complete conversation between the son and the father -- a full repertoire, leaving out not a single detail of the earlier versions.

4. Simeon, Yannai, and the Nazirites

<u>Y. Ber. 7:2</u>	<u>Y. Naz. 5:3</u>	<u>B. Ber. 48a</u>	<u>Gen. R.</u>
1. TNY	1. " " "	1. -----	1. -----
2. Three hundred Nazirites came up in the days of Rabbi Simeon b. S.	2. " " " [Omits <u>Rabbi</u>]	2. -----	2. " " "
2.* One hundred fifty he found grounds for absolution (MS PTH), and one hundred fifty he did not find grounds for absolution	2.* " " " <u>they</u> found	2.* -----	2.* " " "

3.	He came to Yannai the King	3.	" " "	3.	-----	3.	" " " went up (SLQ)
4.	He said to him, There are here three hundred Nazirites requiring nine hundred sacrifices	4.	" " "	4.	-----	4.	" " "
5.	So (L) you give half from yours, and I half from mine	5.	[Omits L]	5.	-----	5.	[As y. Naz.]
6.	He sent him four hundred fifty	6.	" " "	6.	-----	6.	Yannai gave half
7.	An evil report went forth and said to him	7.	" " "	7.	-----	7.	" " "
8.	He gave nothing of his own.	8.	" " "	8.	-----	8.	" " "
9.	Yannai the King heard and was angry. Simeon b. S. was frightened and fled.	9.	" " "	9.	-----	9.	[Omits: Yannai-angry]
10.	After some days important men came up from the Kingdom of	10.	" " "	10.	----- [Begins:] Yannai the King and the Queen were eating	10.	" " "

Persia to
Yannai the
King.

together.
Since he had
killed the
rabbis, there was
no one to bless
for them. He said
to his wife, Who
will give us a man
to bless for us?
She said to him,
Give me your
oath that if I
bring you a man,
you will not
torment him. He
gave his oath and
she brought him
Simeon b. S. her
brother

11. When they were seated eating, they said to him, We remember that there is here a certain old man and he said before us words of wisdom.	11. " " "	11. -----	11. at the table of Yannai the King " " "
12. Let him teach for us a matter (WBD).	12. " " "	12. -----	12. -----
13. They said to him, Send and bring him	13. " " "	13. -----	13. He said to his sister, Send, bring him
14. He sent and gave him [his] word	14. " " "	14. [As above]	14. " " "

15. He came and   15. " " "   15. He seated him   15. " " "
    he sat between   between him and
    the king and   her
    the queen.

16. He said to   16. " " "   16. -----   16. He said to him,
    him, Why did   What is this
    you deceive me?

17. He said to   17. " " "   17. -----   17. [Follows 19]
    him, I did not
    deceive you.

18. You from your   18. " " "   18 -----   18. [Follows 19]
    money and I
    from my Torah

19. As it is   19. " " "   19. -----   19. [Quotes Ben
    written Qoh.   Sira.]
    7:12

                                                              19* [Now come 17 and
                                                                  18]

                                                              19**Why did you not
                                                                  tell me? If I told
                                                                  you, you would
                                                                  not have done it.

20. He said to   20. " " "   20. -----   20. " " "
    him, And why
    did you flee?

21. He said to him,   21. " " " [Omits: 21. -----   21. " " "
    I heard that my   wanted to]
    lord was angry
    against me, and
    I wanted to
    fulfill this
    Scripture, Is.
    26:20

22. And he read concerning him Qoh. 7:12b	22. " " "	22. -----	22. -----
23. He said to him, And why did you sit between king and queen.	23. " " "	23. You see how much honor I pay you?	23. -----
24. He said to him, In the Books of Ben Sira it is written [etc.] (11:1)	24. Book of Bar Sira " " "	24. It is not you that honors me, but the Torah honors me, as it is written Prov. 4:8	24. -----
24* -----	24* -----	24* He said to her, Do you see he does not accept authority.	24* -----
25. He said to him, Give him the cup so he will bless	25. " " "	25. " " "	25. Mixed cup, said to him, bless
26. He took the cup and said	26. " " "	26. He said to him, How shall I bless? Blessed is he whose [gift] Yannai and his companions have eaten?	26. " " "
27. Let us bless the food which Yannai and his companions have eaten	27. " " "	27. [As above]	27. I never heard this from you before

28. He said to him, To such an extent are you in your stubbornness?	28. " " "	28. [See 24*]	28. -----
29. He said to him, What should I say, For the food which we have not eaten?	29. " " "	[29. As above, no. 26]	29. " " "
30. He said, Give him to eat. He ate.	30. " " "	30. He drank it [the cup] they brought him another cup and he blessed.	30. " " "
31. and said, Let us bless the food which we have eaten	31. " " "	31. -----	31. " " "

Gen. R. does not greatly differ from the Palestinian versions. The order of some of the elements changes, and there are a few minor changes in word-choice, not here indicated. But for the rest, we may regard Gen. R. as a fairly accurate representation of the Palestinian Talmud's accounts. There also are some differences in grammar and spelling between the two Palestinian versions. They have not been signified.

The real comparison is between the three Palestinian versions and the Babylonian one. The latter shows how material would be reshaped by an editor for the purposes of legal discussion. The version in b. Ber. omits all reference to elements extraneous to the inquiry of that discussion. It therefore drops the Nazirites and thus loses the explanation provided by that incident for Simeon's absence. The more generalized since he had killed the rabbis make up the difference. The Babylonian tradition further omits all conversations related to earlier incident with the Nazirites. The honor paid to Simeon is now credited to the king, rather than having Simeon take the place of honor on his own. This certainly improves matters and permits an even better sermon to make much the same point. Proverbs replaces Ben Sira, which is consistent with the Babylonian rabbinic denigration of Ben Sira. Finally the story of the blessing is repeated, in the established form, except here, Simeon drinks the first cup, and they have to provide a second. But the explanation of his action is the same; so the argument has been converted into a dramatic gesture.

CHAPTER FIVE
SHEMAIAH AND ABTALION

1. Splitting the Sea

Mekh. of R. Ishmael		Mekh. of R. Simeon b. Yohai
1.	Shemaiah says,	1. " " "
2.	Worthy is the faith that Abraham their father believed in me	2. [omits HY] the [faith], their father
3.	that I shall open for them (LHM) the sea	3. I am opening for them (LHN)
4.	as it is said, Gen. 15:6	4. [Omits as it is said]
5.	Abtalion says,	5. " " "
6.	Worthy is the faith that they believed in me	6. [Same changes as above, no. 2] that Israel in Egypt believed
7.	that I should open for them the sea	7. [Same changes as above, no. 3]
8.	as it is said, Ex. 4:31	8. " " "

The Mekhilta of R. Simeon b. Yohai exhibits fixed stylistic differences from the Mekhilta of R. Ishmael. No. 6 represents a considerable clarification. The point of Abtalion is that their faith, not merely that of the fathers, is being rewarded. Hence Mekhilta of R. Simeon b. Yohai stresses this by supplying Israel in Egypt in place of the less precise they. The versions are otherwise very close and the differences merely stylistic. The Ishmael-version is older.

2. Weavers quote Shemaiah and Abtalion

M. Ed. 1:3-4	Tos. Ed. 1:3	b. Shab. 15a
1. Hillel says, A <u>hin</u> of drawn-water spoils the <u>miqveh</u>	1. " " " [Adds:] <u>a full</u> <u>hin</u> of <u>twelve log</u> " " "	1. " " "
2. But (LS) a man is obligated to say in the language of his master	2. -----	2. <u>for</u> a man " " "
3. Shammai says, Nine <u>qabs</u>	3. <u>a full hin of thirty-</u> <u>six log</u> " " "	3. " " "
4. And the sages say, Not according to the words of this one, and not according to the words of this one.	4. " " " <u>but three logs</u> <u>of drawn water spoil</u> <u>the miqveh</u> [= M. Ed. no. 6]	4. " " "
5. But until (LDS) two weavers came from the Dung Gate which is in Jerusalem and gave testimony in the name of (MSWM) Shemaiah and Abtalion	5. The story is told (MSHB) <u>that</u> " " "	5. " " "
6. Three <u>logs</u> of drawn water spoil the <u>miqveh</u>	6. " " "	6. " " "
7. and the sages confirmed their words	7. " " "	7. " " "

The measurements thus are as follows:

M. Ed.	Tos. Ed.
Hillel: One <u>hin</u> [= three <u>qabs</u>]	one <u>hin</u> = twelve <u>logs</u>

Shammai: [Three hin] = nine qabs   one hin =   thirty-six logs

Sages: Three logs [= 1/4 hin = 3/4   three logs
          qab]

Mishnah-Tosefta preserve the same relationships:

   3-9-3/4 = 12-36-3

M. Ed. 1:3-4	Tos. Ed. 1:3	b. Shab. 15a
8. And why do they mention the words of Shammai and Hillel to no purpose (LBTLH)	8. And why are the names of their places and their occupation mentioned? Do you have a more lowly occupation than weaving, or a more despised place in Jerusalem than the Dung Gate?	8. " " "
9. To teach coming generations that a man should not insist on his opinion,	9. But just as the fathers of the world	9. " " "
10. for lo, the fathers of the world did not insist on their opinion.	10. did not insist on their opinion in a place where oral tradition (SMWH) is available, how much the more so that a man should not insist on his opinion in a place where oral tradition is available.	10. " " "

In b. Shab. 15a the Mishnah is accurately cited, with only a small but essential improvement. There the strange L becomes S, for. Tos. preserves the story about the weavers as
a separate unit. The sages have already given "their" opinion -- the opinion which in the
Mishnah as in the story of the weavers (MSHB) derives from Shemaiah and Abtalion. Tos.
Ed. thus has the sages' opinion circulate separately from the pericope involving Hillel and

Shammai. I have already remarked on the exculpation of Hillel and Shammai. For the Mishnah what requires explanation is the citation of the two masters, Hillel and Shammai, when in fact their opinions do not constitute law.

For Tos. the problem is different. No one is bothered about mentioning Hillel's and Shammai's opinion when it is not law. It is taken for granted that this may happen. The Tos. story emphasizes the modest origins of the opinion attributed to Shemaiah and Abtalion -- it came from weavers from the poorest district. The sermon is in form much the same. But the "fathers of the world" now are not Hillel and Shammai, but Shemaiah and Abtalion! And the operative element is the availability of an oral tradition (SM^CH). The irony is that Hillel achieved the office of Nasi only because he had such an oral tradition from Shemaiah and Abtalion, yet here ignores it. The irony is underlined in Tos. no. 10. All this is revised by Judah the Patriarch, in his Mishnah, which naturally makes Hillel and Shammai the fathers of the world, and their forebearance the point of the sermon.

Here we may attribute to Judah the Patriarch a clearcut preference for the Mishnaic version of the materials. Hillel, his alleged ancestor, is at the center of things. Judah makes Hillel the example of modesty and humility. The story of the weavers occurs -- presumably there was no other version of Shemaiah and Abtalion's opinions -- but it is subordinated. We may therefore take it for granted that the story circulated separately in the form in which it occurs in the Tosefta. Only afterwards was it revised to serve the purposes of the editor of Mishnah Eduyyot. MSHB is dropped. And so are the significant lessons to be learned from the Dung Gate.

3. Gave Bitter Water to Suspected Adultress

M. Ed. 5:6 = Sifre Num. 7	b. Ber. 19a	y. Sot. 2:5
1. [Aqaviah and sages dispute whether to administer bitter waters to convert or freed female slave. Aqaviah says one does not do so. The sages say one does.]	1. TNY: He would say, One does not cause to drink (MSQYN) the female convert nor the freed slave girl, and the sages say, You do.	1. R. Aqiba said, I shall explain: From one man, the wife does not drink and repeat; from two men, the wife drinks and repeats. And the sages say, Whether from one or two men, the wife drinks and repeats.
2. They said to him, The story is told (MSH B) concerning Khorkemit, a freed slave girl, who was in Jerusalem.	2. " " "	2. Khorkemit will prove it, for she drank and repeated and [did it still a] third [time]. (Drops Maaseh b-).

3. And Shemaiah and Abtalion administered the waters to her.	3. " " "	3. -----
4. He said to them, They administered the waters to her as an example (DWGM HSQWH).	4. <u>and</u> he said " " "	4. -----

As we see, y. Sot. has Aqiba's opposition citing <u>not</u> the Mishnah before us, but rather a quite different reminiscence of, or allusion to, it. The story no longer concerns whether a convert or a freed slave-girl is made to drink the waters. She is not a freed slave-girl at all. Now she is just an ordinary wife, in the situation explained above. We therefore cannot suppose the Mishnah is accurately quoted by the sages opposed to Aqiba. A different, slightly related version is used for settling a separate issue. The kernel of both traditions must be an association of Shemaiah and Abtalion with the administration of the bitter waters to Khorkemit -- who was either a freed slave-girl, or a wife in an especially complicated situation, but not both.

CHAPTER SIX
YOHANAN THE HIGH PRIEST

1. Did Away with Confession

M.M.S. 5:15 = M. Sot. 9:10	B. Sot. 48a	Tos. Sot. 13:10	Y. M.S. 5:5	Y. Sot. 9:11 (" " " = as in y. M.S. 5:5)
1. Yohanan the High Priest did away with (BR) the Confession of the Tithe	1. TNY Also he annulled (BTL) " " "	1. -----	1. R.Yohanan said	1. " " "
2. Also he annulled (BTL) the Wakers and the Knockers	2. -----	2. -----	2. -----	2. -----
3. And until his days the hammer was striking in Jerusalem	3. -----	3. -----	3. -----	3. -----
4. And in his days a man did not have to ask about demai	4. And he decreed concerning demai	4. He annulled (BTL) demai	4. -----	4. -----

- 85 -

5.	-----	5.	for he sent through the whole boundary of Israel and saw they separated only terumah gedolah.	5.	" " "	5.	Yohanan the High Priest sent and searched in all the cities of Israel and found " " "	5.	" " "
6.	-----	6.	As to First Tithe and Second Tithe, some were tithing, and some were not tithing.	6.	" " "	6.	" " "	6.	" " "
7.	-----	7.	He said to them, My children, Come and I shall say to you.	7.	-----	7.	-----	7.	-----
8.	-----	8.	Just as in terumah gedolah mortal sin inheres, so in Heave-offering of tithe and tevel, mortal sin inheres.	8.	" " "	8.	He said to them, Since First Tithe [is] in death and Second Tithe is in the sin of tevel	8.	" " "
9.	-----	9.	He arose and ordained	9.	[= y. M.S. 5:5]	9.	Let a man designate Heave-	9.	" " "

	(TQN) for them: He who purchases fruits from an <u>am haares</u> separates from the Heave- offering of tithes and gives it to the priest		offering and Heave- offering of Tithe and give it to the priest	
10. -----	10. Second Tithe -- he goes up and eats it in Jerusalem	10. [y. M.S. 5:5]	10. and Second Tithe -- <u>he profanes it with coins</u>	10. " " "
11. -----	11. First Tithe and poor man's Tithe -- he who takes away from his fellow must bring the proof	11. " " "	11. and the rest -- poor man's Tithe " " " <u>and let him confess</u>	11. " " "
12. -----	12. What are knockers? Rav Judah- Samuel [as above]	12. -----	12. -----	12. -----
13. -----	13. BMTNYT' TN'	13. -----	13. -----	13. -----
14. -----	14. They would smite it with	14. [y. M.S. 5:5]	14. <u>Yohanan the High Priest said to</u>	14. " " "

	hammers as they do beforehand		them	
15. -----	15. He said to them, Until when are you going to feed corpses (NBYLWT) to the altar	15. " " " TRPWT	15. How long are you going to feed " " "	15. " " "
16. ----- 16. -----	16. NBYLWT? Lo they slaughter them, but TRPWT lest the membrane of the brain be pierced	16.	16. ----- altar [Omits on ground]	16. ----- NBYLWT
18. -----	18. He arose and ordained (TQN) for them	18. -----	18. " " " and made	18. " " "
19. -----	19. rings on the ground	19. -----	19. rings [Omits on ground]	19. " " "
20. -----	20. -----	20. -----	20. for he set up pairs	20. -----

We see that both the Babylonian and Palestinian gemarot preserve substantial expansions of the tradition. The two Palestinian versions differ very little, except in the striking failure of y. Sot. 9:11 to correct NBYLWT to TRPWT, the secondary, therefore necessarily later version. Tos. Sot. 13:10 does make the necessary correction, perhaps a scribal "improvement." The earlier form of the Amoraic material must be the Palestinian version attributed to Yohanan, with the beraita's coming later. The Palestinian form omits the colloquy introducing Yohanan the High Priest's message, My children, come and I shall teach you. The Babylonian further improves the diction of his message, just as... so..., and corrects sin of tevel (whatever that might mean) to in...tevel, mortal sin... which makes sense. The Babylonian prefers to have the man eat his tithe in Jerusalem, while the saying of Yohanan is congruent to Palestinian realities of his day. No one could then go up to Jerusalem. The Babylonian improves on this, by rightly, but anachronistically, setting the whole thing back into Temple times. The Palestinians have him confess he has paid his dues, but this is manifestly dishonest, and the Babylonian drops that detail. The interruption of Judah-Samuel obviously will be absent in the Palestinian version. Then the Babylonian further improves on the brief colloquy, by supplying the detail of what they would do (b. Sot. 48a, no. 14), thus augmenting the Palestinian version's simple he said to them. The Babylonian further explains the legal dilemma, no. 17 lest the membrane, further developing the Palestinian version's no. 17. The concluding detail, no. 19, is augmented by on the ground in Babylonia.

There can be no reasonable doubt that the Babylonia beraita not only comes later than Yohanan's version, but in fact depends, and improves, upon it in numerous details. But we have no grounds to suppose that Yohanan possessed some sort of "very ancient" tradition, or, if he did, that he transmitted it in the language in which it would have been formulated centuries earlier. On the contrary, in effect he did much as did Samuel, but instead of phrasing the whole in his own language, he told a story in standard Mishnaic narrative style. This then became the basis for the still later Babylonian beraita.

2. Heard Heavenly Echo

Tos. Sot. 13:5	B. Sot. 33a	Y. Sot. 9:13
1. Yohanan the High Priest heard from the house of the holy of holies	1. WHTNY: " " "	1. M^CSH S " " "
2. -----	2. -----	2. Young men went forth to do battle at Antioch
3. [See above, 1]	3. " " "	3. And Yohanan the high priest heard an echo coming forth from the house of the holy of holies

4.	" " " [= y. Sot.]	4.	" " "	4.	The youths who made war in Antioch have conquered [in Aramaic]
5.	And they tallied (KWN) that hour and they tallied that they conquered at that hour	5.	-----	5.	and they wrote down that time and set in it the hour
6.	[See above, 5]	6.	-----	6.	and they tallied it that it was in that very hour

In no. 3, y. Sot. adds BT QWL, strikingly absent from Tos. Sot. no. 1. The Babylonian version is furthest from the other two, which are quite close to one another, as we saw in connection with Simeon. The Babylonia beraita has dropped nos. 5 and 6, since the issue is whether or not the angels speak Aramaic, and those details therefore are of no consequence here. Otherwise, the differences among the three versions are not substantial. The Palestinian version no. 5 removes some of the verbal repetitions of Tos. Sot. and is certainly dependent upon it. The Babylonian beraita copies Tos. Sot. so far as it is relevant. But its omissions look deliberate and indicate dependence on the Tosefta version, not an independent formulation or the transmission of a separate tradition.

3. Ended as a Sadducee

B. Ber. 29a	B. Yoma 9a	Pes. R. Kah.
1. TNN	1. -----	1. They said concerning
2. Do not believe in yourself etc.	2. -----	2. -----
3. For lo, Yohanan the High Priest served in the high priesthood for eighty years	3. ...and the eighty that Yohanan the High priest served...	3. Yohanan the high priest that " " "
4. and at the end became (Lit: was made) a Sadducee	4. -----	4. " " "

The beraita of b. Ber. 29a is referred to, but not closely quoted, in b. Yoma 9a. What is
more interesting is the form of the citation in Pes. R. Kahana. There the compiler has
imposed a quite different form from TNN. Now it is they said concerning with the
additional that necessary for the new form. Otherwise it is identical to the beraita and
presumably represents a citation of it. The editor of a midrashic compilation was
prepared to impose his own redactional forms on antecedent materials, even those
attributed to Tannaim.

CHAPTER SEVEN
MENAHEM. SHAMMAI

A.

The only explicit reference to Menahem is in M. Hag. 2:2: "Hillel and Menahem did not differ, but Menahem went forth and Shammai entered in." This enigmatic saying is discussed in Amoraic pericopae, as follows:

[Menahem went forth and Shammai entered.]
Where did he go?
Abbaye said, "He went forth to evil culture."
Raba said, "He went forth to the king's service."
It has also been taught (TNY' NMY HKY): Menahem went forth to the king's service, and eighty pairs of disciples dressed in silk (SYRYQWM) went forth with him.

B. Hag. 16b

Where did he go forth?
Some say, "He went forth from measure to measure (MYDH)."
And some say, "He went against his face (KNGD PNYW), he and eighty pair of disciples of the sages, dressed in golden silk [following Jastrow, read SYRQY instead of TYRQY] that brightened their faces like the saucer attached to a pot."
For they said to them, "Write on the horn of an ox that you do not have a portion in the God of Israel."

Y. Hag. 2:2

The Babylonian pericope is unrelated to other materials in the same context. Raba's saying is expanded in the beraita, or perhaps he cited the tradition contained in the beraita. I assume the eighty pair of disciples is a counterpart to Hillel's, in a beraita also from Pumbedita; perhaps it is a stock-phrase.

The Palestinian pericope, isolated from its setting, is enigmatic. The meaning of "from measure to measure" has been variously explained; I do not know what it means. He went against his face generally is interpreted to mean, he went out unwillingly, but here again, I do not know the philological basis for that explanation. The passages compare as follows:

B. Hag.		Y. Hag.	
1.	Where did he go?	1.	" " "
2.	Abbaye said	2.	Some say
3.	He went forth to evil culture	3.	from measure to measure he went forth

4.	Raba said	4.	Some say
5.	He went forth to the service of the king	5.	He went forth against his face
6.	TNY' NMY HKY	6.	-----
7.	Menahem went forth to the service of the king	7.	-----
8.	And there went forth with him eighty pairs of disciples	8.	He and eighty pair [sing.] of disciples of the sages
9.	dressed in silk (LBWSYN SYRYQWN)	9.	dressed (MLBWSYN) [in] silks of (TYRQY = SYRQY) gold
10.	-----	10.	For they said to them, etc.

The Babylonia beraita has improved the Palestinian Amoraic tradition in a number of
respects. First, the enigmatic language, from measure to measure and against his face,
has been dropped in favor of commonplace and immediately comprehensible expressions.
Second, the beraita changes pair to pairs clarifies SYRYQY and drops the redundant gold.
All of no. 10 is dropped in the Babylonian version. My guess therefore is that the
Babylonian version depends upon the Palestinian one. It seems to me unlikely that the two
traditions developed independent of one another, and in this instance the shorter and
clearer probably improves upon the longer and less lucid. But I do not understand why the
substantial detail of no. 10 should have failed to serve the editor of the Babylonian
beraita. We have no reason to attribute any tradition concerning Menahem to a period
before the circulation of M. Hag., for both Palestinian and Babylonian pericopae begin
with the language of the Mishnah, "Where did he go," although the beraita has hidden that
question in the declarative statement of no. 7. The Mishnah, in its present form, must
have been known to all parties responsible for the foregoing pericopae. On this basis we
must regard all the traditions as efforts to provide glosses for the Mishnah, not as
independent traditions deriving from the period before it.

B.

1. Rules about the Sabbath

Sifre Deut. 203	Tos. Erub. 3:7	B. Shab. 19a
1. When you besiege a city	1. -----	1. TNW RBNN
2. Tells that one offers peace two or three days before making war against it...	2. -----	2. -----

3. One does not start a siege against a city less than three days before the Sabbath, and if they encircled them and the Sabbath happens to be, the Sabbath does not interrupt the war.	3. A camp that goes forth to optional war does not besiege a gentile city less than three days before the Sabbath, and if they began, even on the Sabbath they do not interrupt.	3. One does not besiege cities of aliens (NKRYM) less than three days before the Sabbath and if they began, they do not interrupt (Omits: even on the Sabbath].
4. This is one of three things that Shammai the Elder expounded	4. -----	4. -----
5. One does not weigh anchor (PLG) to the Great Sea less than three days before the Sabbath.	5. -----	5. -----
6. Of what things are spoken?	6. -----	6. -----
7. On a long journey, but on a near journey, one weighs anchor.	7. -----	7. -----
8. -----	8. Thus (KK) did Shammai the Elder expound, Until it falls -- And even on the Sabbath.	8. And so (KN) did Shammai say " " " [omits and]

Sifre contains numerous elements lacking in the two Talmuds, but has no knowledge of Shammai's exegesis of Deut. 20:20. Tos. Eruv. refers to an optional war, while to make a required war one presumably may lay siege at any time. Sifre Deut. is unclear on this point. The detail on the siege is the same; Once the siege has started, it must not be lifted despite the Sabbath. The beraita in b. Shab. follows Sifre in omitting reference to the optional war, but otherwise is identical to the Tos. version, except in leaving out what must have been thought redundant, even on the Sabbath. In this instance it is difficult to argue that the beraita is necessarily later than, and dependent upon, the Tosefta's version. It bears at least one important affinity to Sifre. On the other hand, the exegesis of Shammai is copied, with only a minor omission. I therefore imagine the framer of the beraita depended upon Tos., but has improved on it by generalizing a camp that goes forth to optional war into one does not besiege -- presumably more satisfactory for a legal context. Hence in the balance the beraita must be judged dependent upon, and later than, Tos. The appearance of no. 8 in both is the decisive factor, but the rest of the language is sufficiently close, except for the detail at the outset, no. 3, so that this conclusion is highly probable.

2. Would Not Feed with One Hand

B. Yoma 77b		B. Hul. 107b	
1.	They said concerning Shammai the Elder	1.	" " "
2.	That he did not want to give to eat with his one hand	2.	" " "
3.	and they decreed on him	3.	" " "
4.	to give to eat with two hands	4.	" " "

The two passages in fact are identical. The only differences are in the context in which they are cited. The essential materials exhibit no changes whatever.

3. The synopsis of the story about Shammai and Jonathan b. Uzziel has already been given above, Chapter One.

CHAPTER EIGHT
HILLEL

1. Would Fold Together

Mekhilta de R. Simeon b. Yohai 131.12	Tos. Pisha 2:22	Y. Hal. 1:11	B. Pes. 115a	B. Zev. 79a
1. Ex. 12:8	1. -----	1. -----	1. TNY They said of Hillel	1. = b. Pes.
2. It is a misvah	2. -----	2. -----	2. -----	2. -----
3. Hillel the Elder could fold them together and eat them	3. " " " the three of them " " "	3. [Omits: together... and eat them]	3. that " " them at once (BBTHT) and eat them.	3. = b. Pes.
4. -----	4. -----	4. -----	4. As it is said Num. 9:11	4. MSWM = b. Pes.

The two Babylonian versions are identical, except that b. Zev. 79a adds because (MSWM), a minor change. The version of Mekhilta de R. Simeon is briefest. Tos. Pisha adds the three of them, apparently to clarify what we are talking about. The omission of the Scriptural citation (Ex. 12:8/Num. 9:11) may have necessitated the more explicit statement. y. Hal. 1:1 drops would eat them -- perhaps because it was obvious. The Babylonian versions have entirely lost, or dropped, the exegetical framework of Ex. 12:8, so Hillel's action is no longer an "illustration" or a narrative pertinent to that Scripture. Another Scripture, Num. 9:11, is cited now as justification for Hillel's behavior, rather than as an independent exegesis. The Babylonian beraita-form comes last of all; the composite version of Mekhilta is the clearest version, since it preserves the relationship between the exegesis and the Hillel-story, lost in both Tos. and Palestinian versions. It is interesting to see how the exegetical framework is later dropped, then changed and restored, and the story circulates as an independent biographical account.

2. For Three Things Did Hillel Come Up

Sifra Shemini 9:5	Sifra Tazria 9:16	Tos. Neg. 1:16	Y. Pes. 6:1
1. Lev. 11:24	1. Lev. 13:37	1. -----	1. -----
2. Hillel says, Even if he is in the midst of the water (etc.)	2. Hillel says, LSNTQ NTQ BTWK NTQ	2. -----	2. -----
3. -----	3. -----	3. -----	3. Lev. 13:37
4. -----	4. Priest declares him clean.	4. " " "	4. = Sifra 9:16
5. -----	5. If priests say of clean unclean, and vice versa, perhaps he is clean?	5. " " "	5. = Sifra 9:16
6. -----	6. Scripture says, He is clean and priest makes him clean.	6. " " "	6. = Sifra 9:16
7. -----	7. On account of this matter Hillel came up from Babylonia	7. And this is one of the things on account of which Hillel came up from Babylonia	7. = Sifra 9:16
8. -----	8. -----	8. -----	8. [Contrast and harmonization of Deut. 16:2, Ex. 12:5; Deut. 16:8, Ex. 12:15]

9. -----	9. -----	9. -----	9. And he expounded and agreed and went up and received law.

Sifra Shemini has nothing to do with the other materials. Sifra Tazria and Tos. Neg. nos. 4-7 are identical, except that in no. 7, Tos. makes the thing into one of the things, without listing others. The revision may reflect knowledge of a tradition about other "reasons" for Hillel's migration, part of the tendency that Hillel came up and restored the Torah to Palestine. Or, alternatively, the subscription is a stock-phrase. y. Pes. makes one of the things into three things, copies Sifra Tazria word for word, and then adds, for the other two things, the conventional harmonizing exegeses (no. 8). At the end comes a new subscription (no. 9). This phrase makes no sense at all outside of the context of the Bene Bathyra stories, to which the pericope is loosely attached in y. Pes. So y. Pes. no. 9 is a redactional device, external to the pericope and linking it to the antecedent materials in context. Clearly the tradition on the thing/things/three things on account of which Hillel came up has been garbled. Some such list must have existed, perhaps centered on purity laws and/or Passover rules for the Temple. But in the versions that have reached us, we cannot find equivalents to the purity law materials (nos. 4-6), and the others were probably added later, with the awkward subscription supplied at the very end of the process to give some semblance of order to the Palestinian version and to tie it to the foregoing materials in y. Pes. about Hillel's rise to power.

3. Redeem Property at End of Year

Sifra Behar 4:8	M. Arakh. 9:4	B. Git. 74b
1. [Lev. 25:30 alluded to:] LSMYTWT	1. When the day of the completion of the twelve months comes and it is not redeemed, it was permanently sold to him. It is all the same for one who buys and one to whom it is given as a gift, as it is said LSMYTWT.	1. -----
2. To include one who gives a gift	2. [as above]	2. -----

3.	At first he would hide on the day of the twelve months [completion] so it would be permanently sold (HLWTH) to him.	3.	" " "		3.	TNN HTM " " "
4.	Hillel the Elder ordained	4.	" " "		4.	" " "
5.	that he should assign his coins in the Temple fund (LYSKH) and he would break down the door and enter.	5.	" " "		5.	" " "
6.	Whenever he wants, that one will come and take his coins	6.	" " "		6.	" " " [HLZ of Sifra becomes HLH; adds: <u>and</u> whenever]

The minor change in no. 6 of b. Git., supplying <u>and</u>, clarifies the subject of the verb wants. Setting <u>whenever</u> apart from <u>enter</u>, we now are clear that it is the <u>purchaser</u> who can choose the time, not the <u>redeemer</u> of the property. But this was not unclear in the earlier versions, which had supplied <u>that one</u> (HLZ, HLH) to clarify the same issue. Once the Sifra version was fixed, it was cited with practically no modification. The only important changes are in no. 1; the Mishnah superscription conforms to the normal Mishnaic conventions, but the Hillel story is unaffected.

Sifre Deut. 113	Midrash Tannaim p. 80	M. Shev. 10:3-4 (cited b. Git. 36a)	M. Git. 4:3
1. Deut. 15:3	1. " " "	1. <u>Prozbul is not released. This is one of the things that Hillel the Elder ordained.</u>	1. -----
2. But not he who gives his mortgages to the court.	2. " " "	2. -----	2. -----

3.	From here they said	3.	" " [Omits: they said]	3.	-----	3.	-----
4.	Hillel ordained the prozbul.	4.	" " "	4.	-----	4.	" " "
5.	On account of the order of the world.	5.	-----	5.	-----	5.	" " "
6.	That [for] he saw the people, that they held back from lending to one another.	6.	-----	6.	[Omits: that] When " " "	6.	-----
7.	And they transgressed against what is written in the Torah.	7.	-----	7.	and were transgressing + Deut. 15:9	7.	-----
8.	He arose and ordained the prozbul.	8.	-----	8.	" " " [Omits: arose and]	8.	-----
9.	And this is the formula of the prozbul	9.	-----	9.	" " "	9.	-----
10.	I give to you, so-and-so and so-and-so, the judges that are in such-and-such a place, every debt which I have, that I may collect it	10.	-----	10.	" " "	10.	-----

whenever I
want, and the
judges seal
below, or the
witnesses.

| 11. ----- | 11. And thus ex-
pounded Hillel:
Deut. 15:3 --
but not he who
gives his mort-
gages to the
court. | 11. ----- | 11. ----- |

As we observed above, Sifre Deut. 113 combines two versions of the reason and basis for Hillel's ordinance, an exegesis of Deut. 15:3 and the order of the world. Midrash Tannaim preserves the former, nos. 1-4, with practically no variations. M. Shev. preserves the latter, but now supplies Deut. 15:9 as a proof-text; the proof-text has already provided the outline of the historical "event" which Hillel had observed. M. Shev. 10:3-4 knows nothing of the exegesis of Deut. 15:3; the gemara in y. Shev. 10:2 raises the question of how Hillel could have ordained a law in contravention of the Torah. M. Git. 4:3 is a brief summary of nos. 4-5. Midrash Tannaim explicitly attributes to Hillel the anonymous exegesis cited in nos. 1-2.

5. Forbade Interest in Kind

M.B.M. 5:9	Tos. B.M. 6:10	B. Shab. 148b
1. Man should not say to fellow, Lend me a kor of wheat, and I shall give you at the harvest, but he says to him, Lend me until my son will come, or until I find the key.	1. A man says to his fellow, Lend me a keg of wine until my son comes, or until I open the cistern. If he had a jar in the middle of the cistern and the cistern was opened and it fell and broke, even though he is liable, it is permitted.	1. -----
2. And Hillel prohibits	2. " " "	2. -----
3. And so would Hillel say:	3. -----	3. DTNN " " "

4. A woman may not lend a   4. -----   4. " " "
   loaf to her neighbor until
   she determines its value
   in money, lest wheat
   increase in price and they
   be found coming into the
   hands of usury.

The Toseftan version preserves Hillel's prohibition (no. 2) but <u>not</u> the case to which no. 2 refers in the Mishnah, and drops nos. 3-4 entirely. b. Shab. 148b simply preserves part of the Mishnah, without significant variation.

6. Scatter/Gather

<u>Tos. Ber. 6:24</u>	<u>Y. Ber. 9:5</u>	<u>B. Ber. 63a</u>
1. Hillel the Elder says	1. " " "	1. TNY': Hillel the Elder says
2. When (BSCT) they are gathering (KNS), scatter (PZR)	2. " " " (adds d to KNS), scatter (BDR)	2. B^CST HMKNYSYN PZR (as Tos. Ber.)
3. When they are scattering, gather.	3. " " " (BDR)	3. B^CST HMPZR YM (As Tos. Ber.) " " "
4. When you see that the Torah is beloved on all Israel and all are rejoicing in it, you be scattering in it, as it is said, Prov. 11:24	4. And so Hillel would say, If you have seen " " " (BDR) [Omits Prov. 11:24]	4. If you have seen a generation upon whom the Torah is not beloved, scatter, as it is said, Prov. 11:24.
5. When you see that the Torah is forgotten from Israel, and not everyone is paying attention to it, you be gathering it in, as it is said Prov. 119:126.	5. And if not, gather	5. And if you have seen a generation upon whom the Torah is not beloved, gather, as it is said Prov. 119:126.

The Babylonian beraita is based upon the Tos. version, and in some ways improves it.
First, the duplicated verbs of Tos. Ber. no. 5 are made into a single, strong image; then
the conclusion is imperative, rather than participial, so that the reversed condition of no.
4, which in y. Ber. is simply a brief allusion, is neatly spelled out in concise language. No.
4 adds generation. The possibility of the Torah's being forgotten is not raised in the
Babylonian beraita. The Tosefta may contain an echo of the Hiyya-saying that when the
Torah was forgotten in Israel, Ezra, Hillel, and Hiyya restored it, but here the message is
that, if it is forgotten, one should not get involved. The transformation of the verbal
participles of Tos. Ber. to substantive participles in b. Ber. may not be of consequence.
The Palestinian version presents an abbreviated version of Tos. I assume all three
versions are interdependent. Since the interdependence is not merely thematic but
verbal, b. Ber. 63a is almost certainly a careful revision of Tos. Ber.; but y. Ber. is more
of a rough precis. As usual, the Babylonian beraita exhibits considerable stylistic
improvements over earlier versions.

7. Pesah Overrides Sabbath -- Rise to Power

Tos. Pisha 4:13	Y. Pes. 6:1	Y. Shab. 19:1	B. Pes. 66a-b
1. One time	1. This law was hidden from the Elders of Bathyra. " " "	1. -----	1. TNW RBNN. [As y. Pes.]
2. the four-teenth coincided with the	2. " " " and they did not know whether the pesah overrides the Sabbath or not.	2. -----	2. " " " [As y. Pes.]
3. They asked Hillel the Elder	3. They said, There is here a certain Babylonian and his name is Hillel the Babylonia, who served Shemaiah and Abtalion, knows whether pesah overrides the Sabbath or	3. -----	3. [As y. Pes. with glosses, e.g. two great men of the generation, S + A etc. Drops perhaps-him.]

not. Perhaps
There will be
profit from him.
They sent and
called him.
They said to
him, Have you
ever heard when
the fourteenth
coincides with
the Sabbath
whether it
overrides the
Sabbath or not?

4. Pesah -- what is it that it should override the Sabbath?	4. [As above]	4. -----	4. [As y. Pes.]
5. He said to them,	5. " " "	5. -----	5. [As y. Pes.]
6. Do we have one pesah in the year that overrides the Sabbath?	6. " " "	6. -----	6. [As y. Pes.]
7. Many more than three hundred pesahs do we have in the year and they override the Sabbath	7. Do not many " " " Some teach, 100, 200, 300, etc.	7. -----	7. More than two hundred.
8. All the courtyard collected against him.	8. They said, We have already said, If there is with you profit.	8. -----	8. They said to him, How do you know [Here follows heqqesh and qal vehomer]

			Forthwith they seated him at the head and appointed him nasi over them. He was expounding all day long in the laws of the pesah. [After no 27, follow y. Pes. arguments against his proofs, in the form A master said.]
9. He said to them, Tamid is a community sacrifice and pesah is a community sacrifice.	9. He began expounding to them from heqqesh, qal vehomer, and gezerah shavah. " " "	9. -----	[9. As summarized above.]
10. Just as the Tamid is a community sacrifice and overrides the Sabbath	10. " " "	10. -----	[10. As summarized above.]
11. So the pesah is a community sacrifice and overrides the Sabbath	11. " " "	11. -----	[11. As summarized above.]
12. Another thing	12. From qal vehomer [See Tos. Pisha No. 17]	12. -----	

13. Concerning Tamid, In its season is said	13. From gezerah shavah " " "	13 -----	[13. As summarized above.]
14. and concerning pesah, In its season is said	14. " " "	14. -----	[14. As summarized
15. Just as Tamid, concerning which In its season is said, overrides the Sabbath	15. " " "	15. -----	[15. As summarized above.]
16. So pesah, concerning which In its season is said, overrides the Sabbath	16. " " "	16. -----	[16. As summarized above.]
17. And furthermore, qal vehomer	17. [See above, No. 12]	17. -----	[17. As summarized above.]
18. Tamid, that one is not liable for cutting off, overrides the Sabbath, pesah, that one is liable for cutting off, is it not logical that it should override the Sabbath?	18. " " " They said to him, We have already said, If there is [not] profit from the Babylonian. [Here y. Pes. supplies arguments against the foregoing proofs, in direct address, e.g. Heqqesh, that you said,	18. -----	[18. As summarized above.]

has a reply
etc.]

19. And furthermore, I have received from my masters that pesah overrides the Sabbath	19. Even though he was sitting and expounding for them all day, they did not accept [proof] from him until he said to them, May [evil] come on me, Thus have I heard from Shemaiah and Abtalion.	19. -----	[10. As summarized above.]
20. And not the first Pesah but the second pesah and not the community but the individual pesah.	20. -----	20. -----	20. -----
20'. -----	20'. When they heard thus from him, they arose and appointed him nasi over them. He began to criticize them [for not having studied with S + A, and therefore he forgot his law.]	20'. -----	20'. -----
21. The said to him, What will be for the	21. " " "	21. They asked Hillel the Elder " " "	21. -----

people who
have not
brought knives
and <u>pesahs</u> to
the sanctuary?

22. He said to
them, Let
them alone.
The holy
spirit is upon
them. If they
are not
prophets, they
are sons of
prophets.

22. <u>I heard this</u>
<u>law and for-</u>
<u>got but</u> " " "

22. [As y. Pes.]

22. [As y. Pes.]

23. What did
Israel do in
that hour?

23. -----

23. -----

23. <u>The next day</u>

24. Whoever had
as his <u>pesah</u>
a lamb hid it
in its wool,
a goat, tied
it between
its horns

24. " " "

24. <u>Forthwith</u>
" " "

24. " " "

25. And they
brought
knives and
<u>pesahs</u> to the
sanctuary and
slew their
<u>pesahs</u>.

25. " " "
[Omits <u>and --</u>
<u>pesahs.</u>]

25. " " "

25. " " "

26. On that very
day they ap-
pointed Hillel
<u>nasi</u> and he
would teach to

26. [See 20'
above.]

26. -----

26. -----

them concern-
ing the laws
of pesah.

27. -----	27. When he saw	27. " " "	27. " " "
	the deed, he		
	remembered the		
	law. He said,		
	Thus have I		
	heard from		
	Shemaiah and		
	Abtalion.		

y. Shab. has taken nos. 21-2 and 24-7 and introduced the whole with they asked. y.
Pes. is a considerable expansion of Tos. Pisha, which knows nothing of the Bene Bathyra,
has heard not a word about Hillel's studies with Shemaiah and Abtalion, and does not have
Hillel forget the law, but rather introduces the little story about the people as prophets
(or good deceivers) by supposing the Hillel had given a law today, but what can the people
do to keep it tomorrow? The arguments in the three versions are pretty much the same:
qal vehomer, heqqesh, and gezerah shavah.

The important developments come between Tosefta and Palestinian Talmud. The
Babylonian version in general follows the Palestinian, with various glosses indicating that
it depends upon it; it occasionally improves the order. In dropping the refutations of
Hillel and allowing Hillel to take office upon the conclusion of his successful arguments,
the Babylonian version provides a more continuous narrative; but then Hillel's own proofs,
and not his citation of his masters, are made the cause of his elevation to power. The
order is Tosefta, Palestinian Talmud, Babylonian Talmud.

8. Come to My House

Tos. Suk. 4:3	B. Suk. 53a	Y. Suk. 5:4
1. Hillel the Elder	1. TNY'	1. [In Aramaic] Hillel the
says	They said concern-	Elder, when he saw
	ing Hillel the	them acting with pride,
	Elder: When he was	he would say to them, If
	rejoicing at the Re-	we are here who is here,
	joicing of the Place	and does he need our
	of Drawing, he said,	praise? And is it not
	If I am here, all are	written Dan. 7:10. When
	here [alternatively:	he saw them acting
	The Whole is here]	properly he would say,
	and if I am not here,	If we are not here, who

	who is here? He used to say thus	is here, for [in Hebrew] even though there are before him many praises, beloved is the praise of Israel before him more than all. What is the reason? II Sam. 23:2, Ps. 22:3
2. To the place which may heart loves, there my feet lead me.	2. " " "	2. -----
3. If you will come to my house, I shall come to your house.	3. " " "	3. -----
4. If you will not come to my house, I shall not come to your house	4. " " "	4. -----
5. As it is said Ex. 20:24	5. " " "	5. -----
6. -----	6. Also he saw a skull that floated on the face of the water. He said to it, [in Aramaic] Because you drowned, they drowned you, and those that drowned you will be drowned.	6. -----

Tos. Suk. is the simplest version, but is not tied to the celebration of the Festival. y.
Suk., by contrast, invents a "historical" event: When Hillel saw the people misbehaving,
he rebuked them, saying their presence means nothing. But when he saw them behaving
properly, he praised them, saying their presence means everything. In b. Suk, this is
turned from first person plural, and historical, into first person singular, and gnomic. The
Scriptures are dropped, and the whole has, or is given, a theological-mystical echo.
Indeed, without reference to y. Suk we should have imagined the original saying to be a

mystical sentiment said by Hillel (in behalf of God). b. Suk. also preserves the saying attached to Ex. 20:24, and adds a still further saying. Thus b. Suk. has taken Tos. Suk. and introduced it with a double introductory formula (TNY', 'MRW ^{C}LYW); it has the same apophthegm as y. Suk.; but, left in the singular, the saying has no historical or narrative function. Then b. Suk. tacks on another Hillel-saying. y. Suk is entirely unrelated to Tos. Suk., and b. Suk. stands between the two. But I am not sure that b. Suk. no. 1 necessarily comes before y. Suk. no. 1. The relations between the two versions are clear, but the implications of those relations are not obvious to me.

9. Expounded Ketuvah

Tos. Ket. 4:9	Y. Yev. 15:3	Y. Ket. 4:8	B. B.M. 104a
1. Hillel the Elder expounded language of common folk (HDYWT).	1. " " "	1. " " "	1. would expound DTNY'
2. When the sons of Alexandria would betrothe women	2. They would write in Alexandria, for one of them would betrothe a woman.	2. [= y. Yev.]	2. The men of Alexandria would betrothe their wives, and when they entered the canopy, others come and seize them from them.
3. One came and seized her from the market	3. and his fellow " " "	3. [= y. Yev.]	3. [See No. 2 above]
4. And the deed came before the sages.	4. and when " " "	4. [= y. Yev.]	4. -----
5. They sought to make their sons mamzerin	5. " " " to make them " " "	5. [= y. Yev.]	5. And the sages sought to make their sons mamzerim.
6. Hillel the Elder said to them	6. " " "	6. [= y. Yev.]	6. " " "

7. Bring out to me the <u>Ketuvah</u> of your mothers	7. " " " [Drops to me]	7. [= y. Yev.]	7. Bring to me the ketuvah of your mother
8. They brought to him	8. " " " the marriage-con- tract of their mothers	8. [= y. Yev.]	8. They brought to him the marriage-con- tract of their mother
9. And written in	9. they found written in them	9. [= y. Yev.]	9. and he found that it was written in them
10. When you enter my house, you will be my wife according to the law of Moses and Israel	10. " " " and the Jews	10. [= y. Yev.]	10. When you enter the canopy be my wife [drops according- Israel].
11. -----	11. -----	11. -----	11. And they did not make their sons mamzerim

The Babylonian <u>beraita</u> improves upon the former versions in every last detail. First, it has provided a new superscription, so the generalized reference to Hillel's practice is followed by an <u>example</u> given the status of a Tannaitic tradition, DTNY'. Then the story is carefully narrated. The problem is not violence in the market, but under the marriage-canopy. The whole is made a singular event, so we are no longer dealing with a generalized situation, but with a one-time happening, as the story-teller has already indicated. In the earlier versions there is confusion on just this point, with a mixture of singular and plural nouns (<u>mothers</u>). Now the problem of no. 5 is not to declare the litigants, but rather their children, <u>mamzerim</u>. This further clarifies the situation, for in the Palestinian versions we are not sure which generation we are dealing with. The actual situation is corrected in no. 10 to conform to the narrative conditions specified earlier. Then no. 11 tells us the outcome of the case, which is omitted in all the earlier versions. Most important, therefore, the story is now made a single event, rather than the description of a generally prevailing situation to which a single court-case is awkwardly attached. But in this respect the improvement is not complete.

The two Palestinian versions are identical. y. Ket. is presumably copied by y. Yev., or vice versa. But y. Yev. no. 2 is garbled, unlike Tos. no. 2. b. B.M. could well be based on Tos. Ket., without the intervening Palestinian versions, for no. 2 of b. B.M. omits reference to what the Alexandrians <u>would</u> write, and follows Tos. Ket. in this respect; the

story of Tos. Ket. is much elaborated in b. B.M., to be sure. Tos. no. 5, their sons, is
preserved in b. B.M. as we observed.

10. Worthy of the Holy Spirit

Tos. Sot. 13:3	Y. Sot. 9:13	B. Sanh. 11a	B. Sot. 48b
1. M^CSH S	1. " " "	1. -----	1. [TNW RBNN: When last prophets died, holy spirit ceased, but would use the echo, for]
2. The sages entered the house of Guryo in Jericho	2. " " " " GDY'	2. Once they were reclining in the upper room of " " "	2. [= b. Sanh.]
3. And they heard an echo saying	3. An echo went forth and said	3. An echo placed on them from heaven	3.[= b. Sanh.]
4. There is here a man who is worthy (R'WY) of the holy spirit	4. There is among you " " "	4. " " " that the Shekhinah should rest on him	4. [= b. Sanh.]
5. But his generation is not righteous (ZK'Y) for it (LKK)	5. " " "(KDYY)	5. " " "	5. R'WY
6. And they placed their eyes on Hillel the Elder	6. " " "	6. sages " " "	6. " " "
7. And when he died they said about him	7. " " "	7. " " "	7. " " " (They lamented him)

8. Woe for the meek man, woe for the pious man, disciple of Ezra.	8. " " "	8. " " "	8. " " "
9. Again they were sitting in Yavneh and heard an echo saying, There is here a man [etc. as no. 4-5]	9. " " " [With same changes as above]	9. " " " [Same changes as above]	9. [= b. Sanh.]
10. and they set their eyes on Samuel the Small	10. " " "	10. " " "	10. " " "
11. And when he died ... disciple of Hillel	11. [With intervening gloss on why he is called the Small] " " "	11. " " "	11. " " "

* * * * *

Y. A.Z. 3:1

1. R. Jacob b. 'Idi in the name of R. Joshua b. Levi " " "

2. upper room of GDYY'

3. [= y. Sot.]

4. There are among you <u>two</u> who are worthy of the holy spirit, and Hillel the Elder is one of them, and they set their eyes on Samuel the Small.

5. -----

6. -----

7. -----

8. -----

9. Again the elders entered the upper chamber in Yavneh and a heavenly echo came forth and said to them,

Y. Hor. 3:5

1. [= y. A.Z.]

2. [= y. A.Z.]

3. [= y. A.Z.]

4. [= y. A.Z.]

5. -----

6. -----

7. -----

8. -----

9. [= y. A.Z. + Eliezer b.

> There are among you two worthy of the holy spirit and   Hyrcanus]
> Samuel the Small is one of them, and they set their
> eyes on R. Leazar, and they were rejoicing that their
> opinion had agreed with the opinion of the holy spirit.

The Babylonian versions supply what may be Babylonian idioms, e.g. the holy spirit is replaced with Shekhinah. Otherwise, the changes are of no consequence, except for the placing of the story into a beraita. The interesting versions are y. A.Z. = Y. Hor. Here we see a new state of affairs. The story is told by Joshua b. Levi. It derives from Eleazar's or Eliezer's school; or the Samuel the Small-version has been revised so as to make room for Eliezer. Hillel is taken for granted. Samuel the Small is moved to Jericho. But at the same time the upper chamber is moved to Yavneh, replacing the better known vineyard, probably because the story is an exact counterpart. Certainly y. A.Z. = y. Hor. depend upon the Tos. Sot.-y. Sot. versions and are not independent, but still separate forms of the story. If so, this is an instance in which the Babylonian beraita evidently antedates a Palestinian Amoraic version of a story appearing in both places.

B. Sanh. adds upper room; the echo comes specifically from heaven; "they" become the sages; and the holy spirit is dropped entirely. The Babylonian beraita depends upon the Palestinian-Toseftan version. The reformulation by Joshua b. Levi is anomalous.

CHAPTER NINE
SHAMMAI AND HILLEL

1. Retroactive Uncleanness of Menstruant

M. 'Ed. 1:1	M. Nid. 1:1	B. Shab. 15a
1. Shammai says, All the women sufficient for them [is] their period (S^{C}TN)	1. " " "	1. " " "
2. And Hillel says, From examination to examination (PQYDH).	2. " " "	2. " " "
3. And sages say, Not according to the words of this, and not according to the words of this.	3. " " "	3. " " "
4. But from time (T) to time [twenty-four hours] diminishes (MM^{C}T) by means of examination to examination [and vice versa].	4. " " "	4. (MM^{C}TT)

The Mishnaic tradition is cited in nearly identical form throughout. That is nearly always the case.

2. Liability of Loaf for Hallah

M. Ed. 1:2	Tos. Ed. 1:11	B. Shab. 15a
1. Shammai says, From qab for hallah	1. ...They said, Let us begin from Hillel and Shammai. Shammai says, From qab hallah [Omits: For].	1. Shammai says, From qab, hallah
2. And Hillel says, From two qabs	2. " " "	2. " " "
3. And sages say, Not according to the words of this, and not according to the words of this, but a qab and a	3. " " " [HYYB singular]	3. [= Tos. Ed.]

- 117 -

half (HYYBYM) are
liable for <u>hallah</u>.

| 4. | ----- | 4. | As it is said Num. 15:20 | 4. | ----- |

Except for the narrative superscription and exegetical subscription, b. Shab. 15a follows Tos. Ed. 1:1 rather than M. Ed. 1:2 wherever Tos. and M. Ed. differ. But the differences are not important. The Mishnah has dropped the Tosefta's exegetical traditions, as is normally the case. Otherwise the materials are pretty much identical in the several versions.

3. Source of Disputes is Inadequate Study with Shammai-Hillel

Tos. Hag. 2:9 = Tos. Sanh. 7:1 (Yose-logion)	Tos. Sot. 14:9 (MSRBW-form only)	Y. Hag. 2:2 = Y. Sanh. 1:4	B. Sot. 47b = B. Sanh. 88b MSRBW-form) (Yose-logion)
1. When multiplied the disciples of Shammai and Hillel that had not served efficiently (KS RKN)	1. " " "	1. <u>At first there was no dispute in Israel except on laying on of hands only</u>, And <u>Shammai and Hillel arose and made them four.</u> When multiplied the disciples <u>of the House</u> of Shammai and the disciples <u>of the House</u> of Hillel <u>and</u> they did not serve their masters sufficiently	1. " " "
2. They caused to multiply (MRBW)	2. " " " Multiplied (RBW) [qal]	2. <u>and the dispute</u> " " "	2. [= Tos. Sot.]

disputes in
Israel

3. and they were made two Torahs	3. " " "	3. And they were divided into two parties, these declare unclean and these declare clean. And it is not destined again to return to its former place until the son of David will come.	3. And the Torah was made like two Torahs

Y. Hag. depends upon, but greatly augments, Tos. Hag. The two Babylonian versions reject the possibility that the Torah was really divided, therefore add like two Torahs (even though they were really one). The preference for qal RBW rather than Tos. Hag.'s HRBW does not seem meaningful. So Tos. Hag., Tos. Sot., and the two Babylonian versions differ from one another in no important ways, except for one. Tos. Hag. and b. Sanh. insert the lemma into Yose's long saying on the administration of justice, though it interrupts the rhythm and order of that logion, while Tos. Sot. and b. Sot. preserve the saying as an independent lemma in MSRBW-form. Clearly, the saying stood separately and was introduced into the Yose-logion later on, which suggests the explanation for the division of the two Houses comes before the middle of the second century. However, there is always the possibility that the lemma has been inserted into the Yose-materials by a later hand. This was done consistently, however, in both instances of the Yose-saying, which can be explained by later scribal correction. Hence form-critical considerations are hardly decisive in proposing a credible date for the logion.

In this instance, the Babylonian version is independent of the Palestinian one, and depends, rather, on the Tosefta's -- a rare phenomenon in materials we have considered.

4. Lay on Hands: Hillel vs. Shammai's Students

Tos. Hag. 2:11	Y. Hag. 2:3 = y. Bes. 2:4	B. Bes. 20a-b
1. M^{C}SH B	1. " " "	1. TNW RBNN+
2. Hillel the Elder who laid hands on the	2. who brought his whole-offering to the	2. who brought his whole-offering to the

whole-offering (LH)	courtyard and laid hands on it.	courtyard to lay hands on it on the festival.
3. and the disciples of Shammai collected against him.	3. " " House of Shammai	3. " " House of Shammai the Elder. They said to him, What is the nature of this beast
4. He said to them, Come and see that she is female	4. He began to feel (KSKS) its tail. He said to them, See " " " and peace-offerings.	4. He said to them, It is female, and I brought it for peace-offerings. He felt its tail for them.
5. and I need to make her sacrifices of peace-offerings.	5. ----- [Above]	5. ----- [Above]
6. He put them off with words and they went away.	6. " " "	6. and they went away [Omits he -- words].
7. Forthwith the hand of the House of Shammai grew strong, and they sought to establish law according to them.	7. After some days " " " according to their words.	7. That day " " "
8. There was there Baba ben Buta, who was of the disciples of the House of Shammai and knew that law is according to the words of the House of Hillel in every place	8. " " " (Omits: in every place). One time he entered the courtyard and found it desolate. He said, May the houses of those who have desolated the house of our God be made desolate. What did he do?	8. " " " [Omits: in every place.]
9. He went and brought all the Qedar-sheep	9. He sent and brought three thousand goats	9. " " " that were in Jerusalem

and set them up in the courtyard, and said	from " " " and inspected them from their faults " " "	

10. Whoever needs to bring whole-offerings and peace-offerings, let him lay on hands.	10-11. Hear me my brothers, House of Israel, Whoever wants, let him bring whole-offerings and lay on hands, peace-offerings and lay on hands.	10. Whoever wants to lay on hands, let him come and lay on hands

11. They came and took the beast and offered whole-offerings (^CWLWT) and laid hands on them.	[11. As above]	11. -----

For the row 11 CWLWT:

11. They came and took the beast and offered whole-offerings (^{C}WLWT) and laid hands on them.

12. On that very day the law was established to the words of the House of Hillel and no one objected to the matter.	12. " " " and no one said anything.	12. That day the hand of the House of Hillel was stronger and they established the law like them and there was no man there who objected to the matter in any way (KLWM).

The progression from the earliest version, Tos. Hag., to the latest, b. Bes. 20a-b, is in general smooth and routine, except for the substantial intrusion of speeches in nos. 8 and 10 of y. Hag., unavailable to b. Bes. That is surprising, for the accounts in other respects are mutually independent, and the versions in both Talmuds clearly depend upon Tos. Hag. Therefore b. Bes. probably did not have access to Baba's dramatic speeches. I cannot in any other way account for the omission. This also explains why b. Bes. no. 9 does not know how many goats were involved, and why the dramatic, second speech, y. Hag. no. 10, is omitted. So we have an example of what happens when the two Talmuds' versions depend upon the same anterior source, but not upon one another. The differences show that the Palestinians were quite as capable as the Babylonians of creating their own speeches and conversations, and that literary artifice was no monopoly of the Babylonian schools, despite the consistent stylistic excellence of Babylonian beraitas.

Comparing Tos. Hag. with the two Talmuds' versions, we find that both later accounts make Hillel's opposition the House of Shammai adding House of to disciples of. Both add the dramatic detail that Hillel lifted the sheep's tail to show its sex. However,

in y. Hag., he simply supplies the information without being questioned, even hinting at it
through his gesture, while in b. Bes. a dramatic colloquy as usual is introduced: the
disciples <u>ask</u> before he says anything, then he <u>says</u> what it is, and <u>then</u> proves it by
showing them the sexual parts. Both versions drop no. 5, having included the detail in no.
4. b. Bes. leaves out the first element of no. 6. I cannot say why. All versions preserve,
with minor variations, nos. 7 and 8. As noted, y. Hag. has greatly expanded nos. 8-9. All
b. Bes. adds to Qedar sheep is <u>that were in Jerusalem</u>, a normal expansion to add color.
Tos. Hag. is similar to b. Bes. But why b. Bes. then omits the story of what the people
actually did I cannot understand. There should be a clause, as in Tos. Hag., saying that
the people really did accept Baba's invitation and did conform to Hillel's law. Otherwise
no. 12 is unfounded. Hence I imagine the parallel clause has been lost. The conclusion,
no. 12, is everywhere the same, though b. Bes. has rendered it into the Babylonian
<u>beraita</u>-idiom and drawn on no. 7 to supply a counterpart, <u>the hand of Shammai</u> was not
stronger; <u>now</u> it is <u>the hand of Hillel</u>.

5. Uncleanness of Vintaging Grapes for the Vat

<u>B. Shab. 15a</u>		<u>B. Shab. 17a</u>		<u>B. A.Z. 39b</u>		<u>B. Hul. 36b</u>	
1.	He who gathers grapes for the vintage	1.	" " "	1.	" " "	1.	" " "
2.	Shammai says, Ready [to receive uncleanness] (HWKSR)	2.	" " "	2.	" " "	2.	" " "
3.	And Hillel says, Not ready	3.	" " "	3.	" " "	3.	" " "
4.	Except for that instance, for there Hillel silenced Shammai (STYQ LYH HLL LSMPY)	4.	-----	4.	And Hillel (WDY) <u>agreed</u> with Shammai	4.	" " "
5.	-----	5.	Hillel said to Shammai, Why	5.	-----	5.	-----

do they gather
grapes in
cleanness and
they do not cut
olives in
cleanness?

6. -----   6. He said to him,   6. -----   6. -----
                     If you press me,
                     I shall decree
                     uncleanness even
                     on cutting olives.

7. -----   7. A sword was   7. -----   7. -----
                     implanted in the
                     school house.
                     They said, He
                     who enters will
                     enter, but he
                     who goes out
                     will not go out.
                     That day, Hillel
                     was submissive
                     and sat before
                     Shammai like
                     one of the
                     disciples, and it
                     was hard for
                     Israel like the
                     day on which the
                     calf was made.

Nos. 5-7 of b. Shab. 17a stand entirely alone. No. 4 in the other three versions surely
alludes to b. Shab. 17a, nos. 5-7, but b. Shab. 15a = b. Hul. 36b has Hillel silencing
Shammai, contrary to the extended version of b. Shab. 17a, while b. A.Z. 39b has Hillel
agreeing with Shammai! Both certainly are invented on the basis of the subscriptions,
Shammai and Hillel decreed, presumably unanimously. Perhaps b. Shab. 17a, nos. 5-7,
represents a story told to account for that "unanimous" decree. In their present forms we
cannot identify one version as earlier than another. All that seems certain is that the
primary pericope consisted of nos. 1-3, and then was variously embellished to explain how
the decree was attributed to both men when they had disagreed about it to begin with.

CHAPTER TEN
GAMALIEL

1. Ate in Sukkah

M. Suk. 2:5 is accurately cited in b. Yoma 79a, with the following gloss: "Not because the law is so, but because they wished to be stringent with themselves," pertinent to the Mishnah; this comes between Gamaliel-Yohanan and the following clause, about Sadoq.

2. Approved Admon's Decisions

M. Ket. 13:5	Tos. Ket. 12:4	Y. Ket. 13:5	B. Ket. 109a
1. He who agrees on a a sum of money with his [future] son-in-law, and he fled -- let her sit until her head turns white.	1. R. Yose b. R. Judah said, Admon and the sages did not differ where the father agreed for her, that she can say, Father agreed for me, what can I do, etc. In what did they disagree? Where she herself agreed. Admon says, She can say, I thought that father would give to me, now that father does not give to me, what can I do, marry or free.	1. [= Tos. Ket.]	1. [= Tos. Ket.]
2. Admon says, She can say, If I had agreed on my own, I should sit until my head turns white. Now that father has agreed for me, what can I do? Either marry or free [me].	2. -----	2. -----	2. -----

3.	Raban Gamaliel	3.	" " " <u>says</u>	3.	" " "	3.	" " "
	said, I see the						
	worlds of Admon.						

The logion of Gamaliel persists in both versions, M. and Tos. Clearly, the tradition was that he agreed with Admon, but there was disagreement on just what was the opinion of Admon. This means that Gamaliel's opinion in the matter never registered, but was merely a fixed logion pertaining to his opinion of whatever Admon might say. Therefore in all four exempla no. 3 is a stock-phrase tacked on at the end for formal, not substantive, reasons.

3. Banned Targum of Job

Tos Shab. 13:2	Y. Shab. 16:1	B. Shab. 115a
1. R. Yose said,	1. -----	1. R. Yose
2. M^CSH S	2. " " " B	2. " " " B
3. R. Halafta went to R. Gamaliel to Tiberias	3. -----	3. <u>Abba</u> Halafta " " "
4. and he found him that he was sitting by the table of Yohanan b. Nazif	4. -----	4. " " "
5. and in his hand was the Book of Job <u>Targum</u> and he was reading in it.	5. -----	5. " " "
6. R. Halafta said to him, I remember Rabban Gamaliel the Elder, father of your father, that he was sitting	6. -- Rabban Gamaliel [Omits: <u>the Elder</u>] who was standing on the Temple mount	6. He said to him, I remember [Omits: <u>the Elder</u>] that he " " "
7. on (^CL GB) the step on the Temple Mount	7. -----	7. " " "
8. and they brought before him the Book of Job <u>Targum</u>	8. " " " <u>to him</u> the Book Job <u>written</u> [in] <u>Targum</u>	8. " " " <u>and he was reading it</u>
9. He said to his sons [sic]	9. " " " the <u>builder</u>	9. " " " [= y. Shab.]
10. Hide it (GNZ) under the rubble (NDBK)	10. " " "	10. <u>Plaster</u> it (SQ^C) " " "

The Toseftan version has been taken over by the Babylonian beraita with only a few changes. R. Halafta becomes Abba. Gamaliel is standing, rather than sitting (in conformity to b. Meg. 21a); and the concept of genizah is changed, for reasons I cannot tell. But b. Shab. has dropped the whole situation in which the story is told. We are not informed that it is R. Yose, Halafta's son, who reports the story as a criticism of Gamaliel BeRabbi in Tiberias. The story stands as an independent narrative. We are not told which Gamaliel is involved (though the same presumptions apply as elsewhere). His sons become the builder (Lieberman's preferred reading), so the detail about hiding the Targum under the rubble becomes comprehensible. Written is supplied as well. I see no grounds to doubt that y. Shab. is dependent on Tos. Shab., for where the version of y. Shab. does use materials of Tos. Shab. (nos. 2, 6, 8, 9 and 10), it has done so practically verbatim. Then why is the setting of the story so radically revised? Why no specification that it is Gamaliel the Elder? I cannot say, but it is clear that Tos. Shab. has combined two stories, one contained in nos. 1, 3, 4, 5, with the story of Gamaliel the Elder. The combination is smooth and straightforward, and we do not have to doubt that a single tradent is responsible for the whole pericope of Tos. Shab. The parts not appearing in y. Shab. seem to me to have been dropped, not absent to begin with. b. Shab. is somewhat influenced by y. Shab. in no. 6, specifically, but I doubt that b. Shab. has copied that single element from y. Shab.; perhaps the same reasons that caused the tradent of y. Shab. to make Gamaliel stand up and to drop the Elder motivated the Babylonian tradent, but I cannot imagine what those reasons might have been.

4. Letters re Leap Year

Tos. Sanh. 2:6	Y. M.S. 5:4	Y. Sanh. 1:2	B. Sanh. 11b
1. M^CSH B	1. Rabbi Yuda said " " "	1. TNY, Rabbi Yudan said " " "	1. DTNY' " " "
2. Raban Gama-liel and the Elders who were sitting on (^CL GB) steps on the Temple Mount	2. " " " of the 'WLM on the Temple Mount	2. " " " step	2. [Omits and the Elders] " " " step
3. and Yohanan the certain scribe (SWPR HLH) be-fore them.	3. " " " (HLZ) was sitting before " " "	3. [= y. M.S.]	3. " " " (HLZ) was standing before him and three cut sheets were lying
4. He said to him, Write	4. They said to him, Go and write	4. Rabban Gam-aliel said to him, Write	4. He said to him Take one letter and write

5. To our brothers, Men of Upper Galilee, and to men of Lower (THT'H) Galilee	5. Our brothers ('HYNW) " " "	5. " " "	5. " " "
6. May your peace increase	6. " " "	6. " " "	6. " " "
7. I inform you (MHWDN')	7. " " "	7. " " "	7. We inform you (MHWDYN)
8. That the time of burning has come, to bring out (L'PWQY) tithes from the olive-vats	8. " " " Bring out (TPQWN) " " "	8. " " "	8. " " " to sep-arate tithe from the olive vats (L'PRWSY)
9. And to our brothers Men of the Upper South and men of the Lower South	9. " " "	9. " " " [Reverses or-der: South, then Galilee]	9. And take one letter and Write " " " [Omits: Lower South]
10. May your peace increase	10. -----	10. " " "	10. " " "
11. We inform you that the time of burning has come, to bring out tithes from the sheaves of wheat.	11. " " "	11. " " "	11. " " " [As above, nos. 7-8]
12. And to our brothers, Men of the Exile of Babylonia and men of the Exile of Medea	12. " " " and Men of the Exile of Greece and the rest " " "	12. [= y. M.S.]	12. Take one letter and write " " " [Omits: Greece]

and the rest of all the Ex- iles of Israel						
13.	May your peace increase	13.	" " "	13.	" " "	13.	" " " <u>forever</u>
14.	We inform you that the pigeons are tender and the lambs weak, and the time of spring has not come.	14.	" " "	14.	" " "	14.	" " "
15.	And it is well in my view and in the view of my colleagues	15.	" " "	15.	the <u>matter</u> is good " " "	15.	[= y. Sanh. 1:2]
16.	and I have added to this year thirty days.	16.	" " "	16.	<u>to</u> add " " "	16.	" " "

The texts of the letters are virtually identical; the changes are minor, involving a shift from infinitives to finite verbs, adding words here and there. The narrative superscriptions show important changes. b. Sanh. drops <u>and the Elders</u>, which completely misses the point of citing the story: Gamaliel was willing to consult his colleagues, while later patriarchs were not; the antecedent reference to <u>colleagues</u> in no. 15 is lost. The setting of no. 2, however, is standard: the Temple mount. But the <u>steps</u> become <u>step</u> and are moved here and there. Then b. Sanh. supplies some instructions to Yohanan, absent in the earlier accounts. This addition is certainly an improvement of, and based upon, the foregoing versions. It is striking that while the normal changes made in earlier Palestinian versions by the editors of late <u>beraitot</u> do occur, these changes have scarcely touched the substance of the letter.

CHAPTER ELEVEN
SIMEON B. GAMALIEL

1. Lowered cost of Sacrifice

The only important difference between Sifra Tazria 3:7 and M. Ker. 1:7 is in the question of whether the rest of the offerings must be brought later on. M. Ker. (B) says no, Sifra lacks the negative, following M. Ker. (A).

2. Non-Believer and Eruv

M. Eruv. 6:2		B. Eruv. 68b	
1.	Rabban Gamaliel said,	1.	" " "
2.	M^CSH B	2.	" " "
3.	One Sadducee who was living with us in an alley in Jerusalem	3.	" " "
4.	And father said to us	4.	" " "
5.	Make haste and bring out all the vessels to the alley	5.	" " "
6.	before he brings out and prohibits [it] for you	6.	" " "
7.	R. Judah says in another language:	7.	-----
8.	Make haste and do all your needs in the alley before he brings out and prohibits [it] for you.	8.	[No. 10 below]
9.	-----	9.	And the story is told concerning one Sadducee who was living with Rabban Gamaliel in an alley in Jerusalem, and Rabban Gamaliel said to his sons, My sons, Make haste and take out what you are taking out, and bring in what you are bringing in, before this abomination brings out and prohibits [it] for you, for lo, he has annulled his right for you, the words of R. Meir.
10.	[No. 8, above]	10.	R. Judah says in a different language: Make haste and do your needs in the

alley <u>before it gets dark</u> and he
prohibits [it] for you.

The Mishnah has preserved the version of Meir in the story of Gamaliel (nos. 1-6), then
supplied Judah's version in his own name. This is an excellent illustration of Judah the
Patriarch's preference for Meir's traditions. It also illustrates that the Tannaitic
authorities were quite well prepared to transmit legal materials in the form of fabricated
stories, and, without the Babylonian <u>beraita</u>, in this case we should not have known that
M. Eruv. no. 1-6 was in fact a saying of Meir. We should have supposed it was a logion of
Gamaliel II himself. Hence we cannot conclude that words directly attributed to an early
authority in a legal matter or a story pertaining to law must necessarily have been said by
him. The contrary presumption is that the logion is framed to put into his mouth a saying
in conformity with law later on accepted as authoritative.

3. Juggled

Tos. Suk. 4:4	Y. Suk. 5:4	B. Suk. 53a
1. M^{C}SH B	1. 'MR ^{C}WLYW^{C}L	1. TNY' 'MRW^{C}LYW^{C}L
2. Rabban Simeon b. Gamaliel who would dance with eight torches of fire	2. <u>Rabbi</u> " " " torches of <u>gold</u>	2. " " " <u>when he would rejoice at the Re-joicing of the Place of the Drawing</u> would dance with eight torches of fire <u>and throw one and take one</u>
3. and one of them did not touch the ground	3. " " " touch <u>another</u>	3. [= y. Suk.]
4. and when he would prostrate himself (MSTHWH), he would place his finger in the earth of the floor	4. " " " (KWR^C) <u>he would push his thumb into the earth</u>	4. " " " he <u>places his thumbs</u> in the earth <u>and bows</u> (SWHH) and kisses the floor and straightens up
5. bow (SWHH) and kiss and forthwith straighten up (ZWQP)	5. and bow (KWR^C) and forthwith <u>would</u> straighten up (NZQP)	5. [As above]
6. -----	6. -----	6. <u>And no one (else) can do so, and this is Qiddah</u>

The Babylonian Talmud has reworked and improved earlier materials. First, it has
supplied the usual double-superscription by adding TNY'. Of greater importance, it has

added the occasion of the juggling, perhaps implicit in the context of both Tos. Suk. and y. Suk., but not spelled out in either place. Now the juggling is an example of how he would rejoice (lest anyone think that Simeon was like the Magi, who would juggle for thaumaturgical purposes). No. 3 of b. Suk. follows y. Suk.; no. 4 of b. Suk. makes it <u>both</u> thumbs, instead of one; b. Suk. further improves on the duplicated <u>earth/floor</u> of Tos. Suk. no. 4 -- the thumb goes into the <u>earth,</u> and he kisses the <u>floor,</u> then straightens up. b. Suk. further explains that no one else can do such a trick, and a gloss at the end adds that this is the biblical <u>Qiddah.</u> The torches of <u>gold</u> of y. Suk. no. 2 must be a mistake. b. Suk. thus is a combination of important details of y. Suk. (as in no. 3) and the version of Tos. Suk., nos. 4-5, where the word-choices of Tos. Suk. are selected in preference to y. Suk. b. Suk. borrows and develops details in <u>both</u> earlier versions, rather than standing in a single line after the Palestinian Talmudic one. That b. Suk. depends upon the language of <u>both</u> seems to me beyond reasonable doubt. This is not a common phenomenon.

CHAPTER TWELVE
YOHANAN BEN ZAKKAI

1. The Rite of the Red Cow

Sifre Num.	Common to Both	Tos. Parah
	1. His disciples asked	
2. In what garments is the red-heifer done		2. The red heifer -- in what is it done
	3. He said, in golden ...	
4. They said to him, Have you not taught us, our rabbi, in white garments		4. You have taught us in white garments
5. --		5. He said to them, Well spoken, and
6a. What my own eyes saw and my own hands served I have forgotten, how much the more so		6a. A deed which my own hands did and my own eyes saw, but I have forgotten, but when my ears hear, how much the more so
6b. that which I have taught		6b. --
7a. --		7a. Not that he did not know
7b. And all this why? In order to stimulate the disciples		7b. but that he wanted to stimulate the disciples
8. And some say it was Hillel		8. And some say it was Hillel the Elder whom they asked.
9. --		9. Not that he did not know but that he wanted to stimulate the disciples
10. --		10. For R. Joshua said ...
11. But he could not say, What my own hands served		11. --

The versions are close, but by no means identical. The variations of no. 2 are minor and insignificant. Those in no. 4 are of somewhat more interest, for the Tosefta version is briefer and less polite. The real differences begin at no. 5. Tos. 5 is clearly an embellishment of the story. Tos. 6 a deed which is added; Sifre 6b is additional; there is no equivalent in the Tos. version, which leaves the qal vehomer to dangle.

A further clear addition is Tos. 7a, Not that he did not know which replaces all this why with an explication of the problem. 8a is identical in both versions, but Tos. 9 is copied from Tos. 7a, and the intrusion, then exclusion, of Hillel is never actually accounted for. I should regard Tos. 7a-b as a garbling of Sifre 8, 11, which is a coherent statement. Tos. 9 is absent in the Sifre.

In sum, the Tos. version is not only longer than the Sifre one, but also at several points both augmented and more verbose; Joshua's saying is brought gratuitously. I should therefore regard the Tos. version as a later development of the Sifre. Here again we see that what appears in a later document depends upon, and augments, a version in an earlier compilation. The Sifre story not only appears in the earlier document, but it gives indication of being the earlier version.

2. One-hundred-twenty Years

Among the four people, or six pairs who lived the same number of years or died at the age of one-hundred-twenty was Yohanan. The pericope occurs in early and late documents:

Sifre Deut. #357	Mid. Tan. to Deut. 34:7	B. R.H. 31b	= B. Sanh. 41b.	Gen. R. 100:24 100:24
1. Deut. 34:7		--	--	[Begins #7-#13]
2. These are they: Moses, Hillel, Yohanan, 'Aqiba		--	--	[Then:]
3. Moses: was Egypt, 40 Midian, 40 Sustained	worked served	-- --	-- --	lived in palace of Pharaoh, 40 Midian served
4. Hillel: Migrated at 40 Disciple, 40 Sustained, 40	served	--	--	served sages served
5. Yohanan busied Business, 40 Disciple, 40 Sustained, 40	worked served	All the years of Yohanan were one-hundred-twenty Business, 40 Studied, 40 Taught, 40	(see b. R.H. 31b)	worked learned served

			worked as a boor, 40
6. Aqiba Studied, 40 Sustained, 40	studied served sages served Israel		studied served
7. Six pairs lived same number of years	--	--	
8. Rebecca/Kohath	--	--	
9. Levi/Amram	--	--	
10 Joseph/Joshua	--	--	
11 Samuel/Solomon	--	--	
12 Moses/Hillel	--	--	
13 Yohanan/Aqiba	--	--	

The one-hundred-twenty-years pericope thus comes in two versions. In the first, represented by Sifre, Mid. Tan., and Genesis Rabbah, Yohanan is listed among four, then six pairs who lived one-hundred-twenty years. We may further subdivide these versions into two separate units, the "four," then the "six," or in reverse order in the latest version. Sifre and Mid. Tan. are practically identical; the only variations are in the choice of worked for was, served for sustained, in the latter version.

Further, Mid. Tan. corrects the omission in the earlier version of the first forty years of Aqiba's life. The tradition on Aqiba's early ignorance was well-known and widely attested. It would destroy the symmetry of the passage to make no reference to one-third of Aqiba's life, and hence the improvement, which at the same time perfects the saying and cleans up Aqiba's early years.

Gen. R. not only reverses the order -- which is an editorial change -- but elaborates the Egyptian period of Moses, changing the general "in Egypt" to the specific "in the Palace of Pharaoh." Likewise Aqiba's early years are properly characterized as years of ignorance. But for the rest, the account is close to the early versions.

The two beraitot, which are identical, are quite another matter. The beraitot are as follows:

> Has it not been taught, Rabban Yohan ben Zakkai lived for one-hundred-twenty years. Forty years he was in business, forty years he studied, and forty years he taught.

B. R. H. 31b

> Has it not been taught, Rabban Yohanan ben Zakkai lived for one-hundred-twenty years. Forty years he was in business, forty years he studied, and forty years he taught.

b. Sanh. 41b

They ignore all others in the one-hundred-twenty set and concentrate on Yohanan alone. But otherwise the baraita-version exhibits striking similarities to the earlier formulations. The forty-year divisions are repeated. Business (pragmata) is preserved. The disciplehood/sustaining Israel of Sifre Deut. becomes studied/taught, a play on LMD. The beraita cannot be divorced from the earlier documents' version. Rather, it revises the tradition to concentrate on Yohanan alone; of the four/six, YOhanan is singled out. The exegetical framework is dropped as well.

The significant comparison, therefore, is to be made between the version in the earliest document, Sifre Deut., and that in the Babylonian beraita . Are the two versions independent but of equal antiquity? Or has the beraita formulation been extracted from the former and been slightly rephrased? My guess is that the latter has taken place. What was formerly a complete list is now a story about Yohanan alone. The reference to one-hundred-twenty years is the key. Without the exegesis of Deut. 34;&, as well as the list of all those therein included, the reference to Yohanan's exception life-span is meaningless; he could be one of hundreds. The tripartite division of his life-span likewise is pointless outside of the earlier convention. The beraita standing outside of the exegetical framework and the four/six pattern is enigmatic; within that framework, it makes real sense: These were the four/six who both lived a very long time and whose years were equivalently divided.

3. Disputes with Gentiles
The enumeration of the Levites (Num. 4:46) is the common theme in the following:

B. Bekh. 5a	Y. Sanh. 1:4	Num. R. 4:9
Quntroqis asked Yohanan	Antoninus Hegemon asked Yohanan	Agentus the Hegemon asked Yohanan
When Levites are enumerated in detail, you find 22,300. But when counted as a group, 22,000. Where did the 300 go?	In general they lack, in particular they are too many.	Moses your teacher was either a thief or poor at arithmetic. Why?
Three hundred were first-born and a first-born cannot redeem a first-born (Num. 3:44)	The three hundred extras were the first born of the priesthood, and holy cannot redeem holy.	Because there were 22,273, and God commanded: Levites redeem the first-born. Now there were still 300 Levites left over when counted in detail, for we find 273 gave five sheqels each.

--	--	Further, when he sums up the number, he deducts the 300 of the original number. So he left them out so that those 273 first-born might each give 5 sheqels to his brother Aaron.
--	--	or bad at arithmetic.
--	--	Yohanan: he was no thief and was good at arithmetic. But you read but cannot expound Scripture.
--	--	Moses thought, The 22,000 Levites will redeem the 22,000 first-born, and the 300 Levites will remain, and of the first-born another 273. First-born cannot redeem a first born, so when he summed up the number he omitted them because they were first-born.

Num R. has obviously provided a careful spelling out of the reasons for the dispute, in the form of supplied dialogue. The Palestinian version is too brief to have been comprehended without additional explanation. Whether this depended on the Babylonian story or not I cannot say. Perhaps some sort of brief reference was meant to call to mind a well-known, more complete account. But in its current form, without Scriptural references, even without an antecedent for they lack and they are too many, the Palestinian version is garbled. The assertion that Moses was either poor at arithmetic or a thief, of Num. R. 4:9 is borrowed from y. Sanh. 1:4, which concerned not the enumeration of the Levites, but the collection of the sheqel for use in the sanctuary and the final accounting for the use of the money. The passage continues, after some intervening material, in both b. Bekh. 5a and y. Sanh. 1:4, as follows:

B. Bekh. 5a	Y. Sanh. 1:4
And again he was asked	Antonius the Hegemon asked Yohanan

With reference to collection, you count kikkar and 11 maneh.	Moses was either a thief or not good at arithmetic, Ex. 38:27. If a centuarius ... he stole one sixth/one half.

But when Moses gave the money, you find only 100 kikkar. Was Moses a thief or bad at arithmetic? He gave half, took half, and did not return a complete half. Yohanan: Moses was reliable and good at arithmetic. The sacred maneh was double the common one.	Yohanan: Moses was a faithful treasurer and good at arithmetic.

The again he was asked becomes a separate story in y. Sanh., and while the point of both stories is roughly the same, namely that Temple measurements were different from ordinary ones, there is no close relationship between the two accounts. Clearly some sort of common tradition underlies both versions; it had to do with the gentile's ignorance of Scripture and of the Temple's measurements, on the one hand, and of the redemption rules, on the other. But beyond that, I see little in common in the literary accounts.

4. Analogical Exegesis (Kemin Homer)

The homer exegeses occur both with that designation and without. The list in Tos. B.Q. 7:2-5 counts five in all, but as we shall note, there are additional exegeses in the homer-style, both so designated and otherwise. We shall first compare the versions of the five in Tos. B.Q. 7:3-7:

Tos. B.Q. 7:3: Why was Israel exiled to Babylonia?
                          -- no parallels.

Tos. B.Q. 7:4: First tablets, second tablets
                          -- no parallels.

Tos. B.Q. 7:5	Sifra VaYiqra	Y. Hor. 3:2	B. Hor. 10b
--	--	--	Teno Rabbanan
Lev. 4:22	(see Tos. B.Q. 7:5)	(see Tos. B.Q. 7:5)	(see Tos. B.Q. 7:5)
Happy is the generation whose prince brings a sin-	(see Tos. B.Q. 7:5)	(see Tos. B.Q. 7:5)	(see Tos. B.Q. 7:5)

offering for
his unwitting
sin.

| -- | -- | -- | If the prince brings, do you have to ask about an ordinary person? |

| -- | -- | -- | if for an unwitting sin, do you have to ask an intentional sin? |

What is striking, first of all, is that no version of the saying on Lev. 4:22 ever designates
the exegesis as analogical, except for the superscription of Tos. B.Q. The Babylonian
beraita expounds Yohanan's meaning, extending his message. It obviously is a later
elaboration, and once again illustrates the tendency of the Babylonian beraitot to augment
and improve upon earlier materials.

Tos. B.Q. 7:5-6	Mekhilta Neziqin	Y. Qid. 1:2	B. Qid. 22b
And it says Ex. 21:6	Yohanan interprets it kemin homer.	His disciples asked Yohanan	Yohanan would interpret this Scripture kemin homer.
Why ear pierced more than all other limbs?		Why is this slave to be pierced in his ear more than all limbs?	Why is the ear differentiated from all the limbs of the body?
Since it heard from Mt. Sinai Lev. 25:55 Yet it broke from itself the yoke of heaven and accepted the rule of mortals	The ear heard Ex. 20:13 Yet went and stole.	He said to them, The ear heard Ex. 20:2 Yet broke the yoke of the kingdom of heaven and accepted the yoke of mortals	The Holy One, blessed be he said, the ear which heard my voice on Mt. Sinai when I said Lev. 25:55 and not slaves to slaves.
--	--	The ear heard Lev. 25:55 yet went and acquired for itself another master.	Yet it went and acquired for itself a master

Therefore Scripture says, Let the ear come and be pierced, for it did not keep what heard.	Therefore it alone of all limbs will be pierced.	Therefore let the ear come and be pierced.	Let it be pierced.
	--	Because it did not keep what it heard.	
Another matter: It did not wish to be subjugated to its creator, let it come and be subjugated to his daughters.	--	-	--

The version of Pesiqta Rabbati 21 is closest to y. Qid. We see that the simplest version is the Mekhilta, in which Ex. 20:13 is cited. The assumption is that by stealing and being unable to pay recompense, the man was sold into slavery. This version stands apart. Even though it is briefer than Tos. B.Q., we cannot suppose that the latter was built upon it, for the whole exegetical framework in Tos. B.Q. is different.

The comparisons are to be made, rather, between Tos. B.Q. and the two Talmudic versions. We note that the Palestinian version inserts Ex. 20:2 before Lev. 25:55, and omits the "other matter," which seems adequately spelled out in reference to Lev. 25:55 and to require no further repetition. The version in b. Qid. is closer to Tos. B.Q. and I assume it is copied from it, with the inclusion of the kemin homer designation. Lev. 25:55 is further expounded, an improvement on therefore Scripture says. In place of Scripture, the verse is introduced by reference to God, a voice, Mt. Sinai, and so forth; that is, it is made more vivid. The interrelationship between Tos. B.Q and b. Qid. thus is close, but the differences all point toward the latter's being a later development of the former. The account in y. Qid. does not depend upon the Babylonian one, and is a secondary development of the Tos. B.Q. one, also considerably improved.

Tos. B.Q. 7:6	Mekhilta de R. Ishmael
And it says Deut. 27:5 Why was iron prohibited more than all metals? Because the sword may be made from it.	This is what Yohanan says: (see Tos. B.Q. 7:6)
The sword is a sign of punishment and the altar of atonement.	(see Tos. B.Q. 7:6)

Remove something which is a sign of punish-   (see Tos. B.Q. 7:6)
ment from something which is a sign of
atonement.

And it is a qal vehomer: (see Tos. B.Q. 7:6)

Stones which do not see, hear, speak --   (see Tos. B.Q. 7:6)

Because they bring atonement between Israel   (see Tos. B.Q. 7:6)
and their father in heaven.

Scripture says Deut. 27:5.   (see Tos. B.Q. 7:6)

Sons of Torah who are atonement for the world   (see Tos. B.Q. 7:6)

How much the more so that any of all the de-   (see Tos. B.Q. 7:6)
mons should not touch them.

Tos. B.Q. 7:7	Mekhilta Bahodesh	Sifra Qedoshim
Behold it says Deut. 27:6	Yohanan says, Behold It says Deut. 27:6	(see Mekhilta Bahodesh)
Stones which bring peace between Israel and their father in heaven, the Omnipresent says, should be perfect before me	Stones which bring peace.	(see Mekhilta Bahodesh)
	It is a qal vehomer:	(see Mekhilta Bahodesh)
Sons of Torah, who perfect the world	Stones do not see, hear speak.	(see Mekhilta Bahodesh)
How much the more so should they be perfect before the Omnipresent.	Because they bring peace between Israel and their father in heaven, the Holy One said Deut. 27:5.	(see Mekhilta Bahodesh) Scripture
--	How much the more so the one who brings peace between man and man, husband and wife, nation	(see Mekhilta Bahodesh) [Man/man omitted] family/ family, city/city, state/ state, nation/nation.

and nation, family and
family, government and
government.

be protected so no harm should come to him.	How much the more so should punishment not overtake him.

We see that the stones which bring peace and the prohibition of iron appear both together and also separately in Tos. B.Q. 7:6-7. The first version contains the prohibition of iron, and adds to it the stones, the second treats stones alone. The qal-vehomer appears only in connection with stones. Differences between Mekhilta's and the Sifra's accounts are striking, and it is not difficult to assign priority. Revisions of the exegesis were intended to change condemnation of war and swords and praise of peacemakers into praise of study of Torah and disciples of Torah.

5. Because You Did Not Serve

The sermon on the occasion of seeing a starving child exists in a number of formulations, appearing in the earliest to the latest documents. We shall compare the versions by the sequence of documents.

Mekhilta Bahodesh	Sifre Deut.	Y. Ket. 5:11	Tos. Ket. 5:9-10
They were not satisfied to count.	--	[Marta daughter of Boethus had large dowry ...	[The daughter of Naqdimon had a large dowry.
Ezek. 40:1	--		
Hag. 1:15	--	Eleazar b. Zadoq said he saw her gathering barley under hooves of horses in Acre, and I cited concerning her Deut. 28:56 and Song 1:8]	Eleazar b. Zadoq says he saw her gathering barley under the hooves of horses in Acre.
And thus it says, If you know not (Song 1:18)	--		
And it also says, Because you did not serve (Deut. 28:47-8)	--		And I cited concerning her Song 1:8]
Yohanan going to Emmaus saw girl picking barley-corn	Story is told that Yohanan was riding an		

from horse-dung.   ass and stu-
                                dents walking
                                after him, and
                                he saw girl
To disciples: What   picking bar-
is girl?   ley-corn from
                                the feet of
                                Arab cattle.

She is Jewish

The horse belongs to   When she saw
an Arab.   Yohanan she
                                wrapped herself
                                in her hair and
                                stood before
Yohanan to disciples: him, asking for
Now I know meaning of   food.
Song 1:8.

                                She: Naqdimon
You are unwilling to   b. Gurion, don't
be subject to God,   you remember my
are now subject to   ketuvah?
Arabs.

                                He remembers   --   --
You were unwilling to--   ketuvah also that
pay head-tax (Ex. 38:26)   her family went
now pay fifteen sheqels   on carpets to
                                Temple.
--repair roads for
pilgrims now do so   And all my life   --   --
for enemy   I sought meaning
                                of Song 1:8
Thus it says, Because   Read not...
you did not serve
(Deut. 28: 47-8)   For when Israel do
                                the will of the
                                Ommipresent, no
                                one can rule them,
                                but when they do

not, the lowest
nation rules them,
even the cattle of
the lowest nation.

B. Ket. 66b	ARNa chap. 17
<u>Teno Rabbanan:</u> Story is told that Yohanan was riding on ass and <u>going out of Jerusalem</u> and his students were walking after him. He saw a girl picking barley-corn from between feet of Arab cattle.	Yohanan saw girl in marketplace, picking barley from feet of Arab cattle.
	Who are you?
	No answer.
When she saw him, she wrapped self in hair, stood before him, and said, Rabbi, feed me.	Covered self with hair, sat before him, I am daughter of Naqdimon b. Gurion.
He asks, Whose daughter are you?	Yohanan: What happened to wealth of father, father in law.
She: Naqdimon b. Gurion.	Girl: Cites proverb.
Yohanan: What happened to your father's wealth?	Yohanan: Now I understand Song 1:8.
Girl: Cites proverb.	Israel has been surrendered to meanest of peoples, even to cattle-dung.
She: don't you remember my marriage contract?	Girl: Reminds him about marriage-contract.
Yohanan: I remember I signed it.	Yohanan: By the Temple service, I signed her marriage-contract and also that her family went on carpets to Temple.
Yohanan wept and said, Happy are you O Israel, when you do God's will no one can rule you, but when you do not, even meanest people rule you, even their cattle.	--

I have cited the Palestinian Talmud and the Tos. Ket. stories merely to indicate how the same Scriptures are used in several different ways. The Toseftan story may be the earlier of the two, for in the Palestinian Talmudic account, we see a proliferation of Scriptures;

on the other hand, the daughter in the Tosefta is Naqdimon's, in the Palestinian Talmud, Boethus's. The stories are related, but the latter is not simply an amplified version of the former.

The four accounts in which Yohanan appears are certainly interrelated, though the exact relationships are by no means clear. Mekhilta is a play on Deut. 28:47-8 and Song 1:8, while in Sifre Deut., Deut. 28:47-8 does not appear at all. In Mekhilta the girl is unnamed; Yohanan has never met her; the pathos of her fall from prosperity is ignored. The meaning of Song 1:8 is elucidated by Deut. 28:47-8. But the girl's plight plays no intrinsic role. And the disciples play an active part. In Sifre Deut., by contrast, the girl is the central figure, asking for food, then identifying herself, reminding Yohanan about her ketuvah; and he further remembers the luxurious way her family lived. then comes Song 1:8, now the point of it all. Finally comes the closing homily, "When Israel do ..."

Perhaps Sifre Deut. is a development of Mekhilta Bahodesh, in which the detail about the girl becomes greatly embellished, indeed is made the point of the encounter. Then You were unwilling ceases to be an exegesis and becomes an outright homily, independent of a Scripture. But some details of Mekhilta are dropped, first, the conversation with the disciples, second, the location of the trip. When the girl becomes central, the disciples pass out of the picture, serve as a silent audience.

The Babylonia beraita clearly depends upon Sifre Deut. Now the location of the trip is once again supplied. The encounter with the girl if further amplified by the question, What happened to your father's money? This is inserted before the marriage-contract, so the girl now introduces the topic not in order to identify herself, but as a separate colloquy. Srikingly, all Scriptural exegeses are omitted, but the homily of Sifre Deut. is further expanded by Happy are you, O Israel. Otherwise it is identical.

As usual, ARNa is highly literary. The disciples are absent, having no role to play. The marketplace is now the setting. The conversation is dramatic, eloquent. The girl then identifies herself; Yohanan asks about her father's money; she replies citing a well-known proverb. Yohanan now introduces Song 1:8 and the homily immediately follows, in somewhat abbreviated form. Finally, the details of the marriage-contract and the luxurious way of living of her family are tacked on.

In effect, the version of the Mekhilta stands by itself; Sifre Deut. forms the basis for both the Babylonian beraita and the ARNa. The components common to all versions are as follows:

1. Starving girl picks barley-corn from dung of Arabian horses/cattle.
2. Yohanan sees, asks who she is.
3. He cites Song 1:8 in reference to the girl.

Unique to Mekhilta Bahodesh is the further exegesis of Deut. 28:47-8; but the homilies appearing in all other accounts in fact are based upon the plain sense of that very Scripture: "If you do well, you will be blessed, but if not, you will be cursed." The additional elements common to Sifre Deut., b. Ket. beraita, and ARNa, are as follows:

4.   The girl identifies herself as Naqdimon's daughter.

5.   Do you not remember you witnessed my marriage-contract?

6.   Indeed I do, and what happened to your father's wealth? I remember also how your family went to the Temple on carpets.

7.   [Song 1:8 appears in Sifre and ARNa.]

8.   When you do God's will, no one can rule you, but when you do not, you are given into the hands of mean people and their cattle.

We may further conjecture that the association of the unnamed girl of Mekhilta with the daughter of Naqdimon in Sifre and afterward derives originally from the fact that an exegesis of Song 1:8 is common to both Yohanan and Eleazar b. Zadoq, leading to the further assumption that the "you" of "If you do not know" is, in fact, Naqdimon's daughter. Henceforward, the citation of Song 1:8 will remind everyone to whom Yohanan was talking, and further details naturally will be supplied from other stories about her. The association of Yohanan with her father is drawn quite routinely in the escape stories, but these are very late, certainly much later than the materials before us, and I imagine that the escape-stories have been shaped by Because you did not serve materials, rather than vice versa.

The b. Ket. 66b and ARNa Ch. 17 versions of the encounter with Naqdimon's daughter probably are developments of Sifre Deut., which is likely to be related to, but separate from, Mekhilta Bahodesh. Thus stories appearing in documents of approximately the same age do not appear to improve on one another, but do exhibit complex relationships with one another. Stories appearing in later documents as usual seem to be developments of stories appearing in earlier documents. In general, marks signifying a later version normally, though not invariably, include augmentation and other kinds of development. In the historical stories this invariably is the distinguishing trait of the later versions.

PART THREE

THEORIES OF THE PERIPATETIC SAYING

CHAPTER THIRTEEN
"HE OFTEN USED TO SAY"

Among the three familiar interpretations of the fact that a story appears in more than one document and that a saying occurs a number of times, the oldest is also the silliest. If a given saying occurs in numerous passages, then the person to whom the saying is ascribed is alleged to have said that saying a lot. Since the "he often used to say"-explanation circulates in both simple and sophisticated versions, we have to take a moment to "refute" it. Not only in Israeli yeshivot and universities will people yet find such a refutation provocative. But since the theory is just silly, the refutation will prove equally trivial.

The simplest proof that the present explanation cannot serve derives from the fact that two or more stories of an event that cannot have been repeated do circulate in the Talmudic corpus. Since several versions of the same story in the present case by definition report only a one-time event, one which simply cannot have been repeated, it must follow that the explanation at hand has now to leave the stage of rational discourse, though believers, of course, will always believe whatever they find convenient. For the purposes of argument I can think of two never-to-be-repeated events, one, the destruction of the Second Temple, the other, the death of a rabbi. As we saw above, Chapter One, Eliezer b. Hyrcanus dies twice in Talmudic writings. How explain the two versions? No fundamentalist maintains that the Temple was destroyed twice. None to my knowledge (here I am less certain of what is to be found in the dim reaches of the Yeshiva-periodicals) can claim that a rabbi died, was resurrected, then died a second time, allowing for two events, to which two quite different stories of the same rabbi's death may then be made to refer. Since, on the face of it, the theory at hand cannot explain important facts, the theory has to wend its way off the stage of reasoned discourse. A new theory will have to take shape to account for the same facts -- all of them, all the time.

The case at hand involves Yohanan ben Zakkai's escape from Jerusalem during the Roman siege. I think even the most primitive Orthodox and Israeli scholars will concur that Yohanan surely did not escape from Jerusalem one way, crawl back into the city, then make an escape another way -- the one time dealing with one group of people, the next with another, the one time seeing Vespasian and having one conversation with him, the next time seeing Vespasian but having a different conversation with him. So it would appear to me sufficient to point to the following case. We shall leave in ruins the first of the three theories on the meaning of diverse versions of a given event.

To the texts at hand: we have two fundamentally different accounts of Yohanan's escape, each in two versions, those in ARNa and ARNb, and in b. Git. 56b and Lam R. It is obvious that all are very late stories. None can possibly date from before ca. A.D. 200.

In Tannaitic traditions, attributed to authorities before A.D. 200, we find not the slightest reference to an escape. Indeed, we should not know how Yohanan reached Yavneh, if we had to rely on the Tannaitic midrashim, Mishnah-Tosefta, and even the beraitot in the Babylonian Talmud. Nor does the Palestinian Talmud contain a reference to an escape. If we knew the date of The Fathers According to Rabbi Nathan (= ARN), we should probably have a clear idea about the literary beginnings of the escape legend, though the several components of the ARNa account are probably older and now have been reshaped. We may only imagine that at some point after 200, it became important to tell escape-stories; no single account was ever widely accepted. I can propose no conjecture on when, where, or why it became important to make up such a story, or to whom it would have been useful. Perhaps opposition to Julian's attempt, in 360, to rebuild the Temple provoked it, but my guess is that components of the escape-legends are older than that.

The Babylonian version is clearly a composite, while ARN is, as usual, more literary, smoother, but also formed from earlier materials. We shall first compare the two ARN versions, then the second pair, and finally contrast one account with the other.

ARNa		ARNb. Ch. 6, Schechter, p. 10a
I.	Vespasian asks sign of submission.	I. see ARNa
	Yohanan counsels Jews to give it, save the Temple, they refuse.	see ARNa
	Vespasian's men heard of Yohanan's loyalty.	see ARNa
II.	Yohanan tells Joshua and Eliezer to help him escape.	II. see ARNa
	Make a coffin. Eliezer and Joshua carried coffin.	see ARNa see ARNa
	Gatekeepers object, but are told it is a corpse.	Gatekeepers object, want to stab corpse. Disciples reply, You will be said to have stabbed Yohanan's corpse.
III.	Coffin carried to Vespasian, Yohanan rises from coffin before emperor. Are you Rabban Yohanan? What can I give you?	III. Yohanan gets out of coffin, goes and asks after welfare of Vespasian as one asks about a king, saying Ridumani Imperion. Are you Ben Zakkai?

Yavneh, so I may teach, establish prayerhouse, do commandments.

Go.

Yohanan predicts coming rise to
power, citing Is. 10:34.

IV. Yohanan tells Vespasian you are
about to be made emperor, on
basis of Is. 10:34.

Two or three days later, news
came that Vespasian was emperor.

IV. [After his prediction is proved
correct, Yohanan is permitted to
make a request.]

Give me Yavneh where I may teach
Torah and make zizit and do the other
commandments.

Behold it is given to you as a gift.

Parts I and II are practically identical in both versions. But parts III and IV are not. In the
latter, the prediction comes before the emperor gives any favors, as in b. Git. Likewise,
gatekeepers are hostile to the disciples. In general, as we shall see, ARNb combines
major elements of ARNa and the Babylonian version; it is a composite of the two,
standing between them. The Babylonian and Midrashic accounts compare as follows:

B. Git. 56b

Lam. R. 1.5.31

I.   Abba Sikra was Yohanan's
nephew, came to Yohanan.

How long will you kill the
people by starvation?

Abba Sikra cannot help.

Then, Yohanan asks, think of a
plan to get me out. Perhaps
there may be some slight sal-
vation.

Pretend to be sick, die, and he
did so.

I.   Ben Battiah was Yohanan's
nephew. When Yohanan heard his
nephew had burned the city's
supplies, he exclaimed "woe".
Ben Battiah heard, called Yohanan to
him, asked why. Yohanan said
he had praised the burning of the stores
because now the people would
have to fight.
Three days later, he saw people
starving, decided to escape. Asked
Ben Battiah to help. Ben Battiah
says only dead can leave.

Yohanan determined to escape as
corpse.

II.   Eliezer carried one side,   II.   Eliezer and Joshua carried him,
        Joshua the other.   Ben Battiah accompanied cortege.
                                                     Guards wanted to stab body, Ben
        Guards wanted to push, then stab   Battiah said it will give us a bad
        body. Disciples say it will give   name.
        you a bad name.

III.   When he reached there, he said,   III.   Disciples returned to city.
        Peace be to you, O King.   Yohanan wandered among Roman
                                                     troops, asked where king was.
        Vespasian says, You are worthy   Yohanan was brought to Vespasian,
        of death. I am not a king, and   Vive domine Imperator.
        if I were, why did you not come
        earlier.

        But you are a king, Yohanan says   Vespasian: You endanger my life,
        citing Is. 10:34, Jer. 30:21,   for if king hears, he will put me
        Deut. 3:25.   to death.

        I could not come sooner because   But you are a king, Is. 10:34.
        revolutionaries would not let me.

IIIb.   Vespasian asks, If you have   ----- (VI)
        honey and a reptile is around the
        cask, would you not break the
        cask to kill the snake?

        Yohanan fell silent.   ----- (VI)

        R. Joseph/R. Aqiba cites Is.   -----
        44:25. He should have answered,
        One takes tongs.

IV.   Meanwhile messenger came from   IV.   Yohanan put in room without
        Rome, Vespasian is king.   light, but could tell time because of his
                                                     study.

V.   He had one shoe off, one shoe   V.   Vespasian bathes at Gophna, but
        could do nothing.   could not get shoes back on, for word
                                                     came that Nero died and he
        Yohanan says, you have heard   was king. Yohanan explains, You
        good news, cites Prov. 15:30.   have heard good news, cites Prov.

Let someone you dislike pass before you, cites Prov. 17:22.

15:30 and Prov. 17:22.

VI. If you were so wise, why did
you not come sooner?

I already told you.

So did I.

VI. Then they began to speak in para-
bles. If a snake in a cask, what to do?
Yohanan: Charm the snake.
Pangar: Break the cask and kill the
snake. If a snake in a tower:
Yohanan, bring a charmer. Pangar:
Burn the tower. Yohanan to Pangar:
You hurt us. Pangar: I seek your
welfare. So long as Temple exists,
heathen kingdoms will attack you, if it
is destroyed, they will not. Yohanan:
The heart knows what your real
intention is.

VII. I, Vespasian continued, will
soon leave. What can I give
you?

Yavneh and its sages, the chain
of Gamaliel, and a physician for
Zadoq.

R. Joseph/R. Aqiba cites Is.
44-25. He should have asked the
Romans to leave them alone.

VII. Vespasian: What may I give you?

Yohanan: Abandon this city and de-
part.
Vespasian: I did not become king to
abandon Jerusalem.

Yohanan: Leave the western gate
open for refugees.

VIII. After the conquest, Vespasian offered
to save Yohanan's friends.

Yohanan sent Eliezer and Joshua to
bring Zadoq.

IX. Vespasian: Why do you stand up before
emaciated old man.

Yohanan: If we had one more like him,
you would not have conquered

Jerusalem. He lives on a fig, teaches
many sessions, fasts a lot.

Vespasian healed Zadoq.

-----   X. Zadoq's son: Father, give them reward
in this world.

He gave them calculation by fingers
and scales for weighing.

-----   XI. After conquest, Vespasian assigned
destruction of four ramparts to four
generals.

Pangar had western wall, but did not
destroy it.

Pangar explained to Vespasian, I kept it
so people would know what you
destroyed.

Vespasian replied, Well said, but you
disobeyed, so commit suicide.

He did so, and thus the curse of Rabban
Yohanan ben Zakkai alighted upon him.

Lam R. has been corrected in important details to conform to the criticism of b.
Git.; note the comparison of b. Git IIIb and VI with Lam. R. VI and VII. Yet in many other,
equally important respects, Lam R. stands by itself. The Abba Sikra account is now
expanded into two parts. Lam. R. parts IV, VI, VII, VIII, IX, X, and XI have no close
counterpart in the earlier version, though the "physical for Rabbi Zadoq" of Git. part VI
becomes the long encounter of Lam. R. part IX and X.

We have no reason to doubt Lam. R. is later than Git. The former is greatly
elaborated over the latter. The version appearing in the later document is probably later
than the one appearing in the earlier document. Indeed, it is expanded both through
details common to both stories, and with completely new materials. The following
summarizes the points in common as well as the stories found in one account and not in
another:

ARN	B. Git.	Lam. R.
Vespasian asks submission, Yohanan agrees.	-----	-----
Joshua and Eliezer effect the escape of "corpse."	Abba Sikra -- "corpse"	Ben Battiah -- "corpse."
-----	Starvation.	-----
-----	-----	Burning of stores.
Guards went to stab corpse.	(see ARN)	(see ARN)
Meets Vespasian	(see ARN)	(see ARN)
What can I give you?	-----	-----
Yavneh	(see ARN)	(see ARN)
Prediction, Is. 10:34	(see ARN)	(see ARN)
News comes.		
-----	Honey and reptile.	(see b. Git.)
-----	Is. 44:25	(see b. Git.)
-----	Feet bloated, Prov. 15:30, 17:22	(see b. Git.)
-----	Chain of Gamaliel	-----
-----	Heal Zadoq (see b. Git.)	
-----	-----	Yohanan told time miraculously.
-----	-----	Tower and reptile.
-----	-----	Pangar.
-----	-----	Abandon city.
-----	-----	Accept refugees
-----	-----	Why honor Zadoq?
-----	-----	Zadoq gives calculation.
	-----	Pangar fails to destroy Western wall.

All accounts have in common the escape through a ruse, the participation of Joshua and Eliezer, the request for Yavneh, the prediction of Vespasian's coming rise to power on the basis of Is. 10:34, and the arrival of news to verify Yohanan's prediction. Although the order and perspective of ARNa differ from those of the later versions, no important detail in the former is absent in the latter. It seems possible that ARN has served as a source of materials -- though as that alone -- for the Babylonian and Lam. R. stories. I think it is far more likely, however, that some sort of independent materials circulated widely, and were used by the authors of the several stories independently of one another. Otherwise, I imagine, the relationships between ARN and the other stories would be somewhat more like those between b. Git. and Lam. R. There would be signs of development and augmentation, and we see none. Hence some stories, particularly about the escape and prediction (Is. 10:34) probably antedated the formation of the several accounts. To conclude: ARNa stands by itself, quite apart from b. Git. and its later formulation in Lam. R.; we do not know whether ARNa comes before b. Git. Since the two are not directly related, it hardly matters.

One of the truly original and great minds of Talmudic history, G. Alon (in his Mehqarim [Tel Aviv, 1957] I, pp. 238-251) explains the difference between the two escape stories just now surveyed. The sources, Alon says, reveal two traditions concerning Yohanan's escape. According to the first he left the city after the Zealots refused to surrender to Vespasian, because he was opposed to the war and hoped to save the Temple. Vespasian had spies in the city and knew that Yohanan favored his cause. When he came to the Romans, they therefore recognized him, brought him directly to Vespasian, who received him and asked what he could do in his behalf. Yohanan thereupon made his famous request for Yavneh, then prophesied Vespasian's rise to power. According to the second view, Yohanan surrendered not because he opposed the war, but because he opposed the military policies of the Zealots. He favored remaining in the besieged city for a defensive war, rather than making sorties against the Roman lines. The Romans according to this account knew nothing about him, had no special regard for him, and so at his interview with Vespasian he had to justify his actions. Having nothing to his credit, he made a prediction; when it came true, he was granted a small favor.

What is important here in Alon's sensitive analysis is simple. He does not imagine that the two stories tell us about two different happenings. And neither can anyone else — any more. If so, then on the face of it, theories about how "he often used to say," that invoke the same mode of explaining the same phenomenon and parallel phenomena when they occur elsewhere, likewise serve no further purpose. The claim that the sages enjoyed reenacting the scenes of their life, including how they died, for one audience after another, with each statement recorded, each event set down, takes up its lonely vigil alongside the theory of the flat earth and other lost causes of another age. And so we bid adieu, once for all, to the theory of the repetitious rabbis.

CHAPTER FOURTEEN
IN SEARCH OF THE "ORIGINAL" "TRADITION"

The second and third explanations of the presence of diverse versions of a single vent superficially lay claim to be somewhat more sophisticated. But neither leads to a suitable solution to the problem or even to a theory of how to proceed. The one at hand posits that behind several versions of a saying or story lies (1) an "original", (2) "tradition," handed on in linear fashion. I place quotation marks around both words, not because I wish to impute to the words meanings other than those commonly assigned to them. Rather, the reason is that, in context here, I do not know what they mean.

By "original" one may mean the original version of a <u>tradition</u> later on elaborated. But one may also mean the original <u>saying</u>, as the person to whom it is attributed really said it. These represent quite different claims.

By "tradition" people commonly mean a story that has been made up <u>and handed on in linear succession</u> over a period of time. Hence if we refer to a "tradition" in the Mishnah or in the Bavli, we are properly understood to claim that a saying or story, made up earlier, has reached the Mishnah or the Bavli through a continuous, linear process of handing on, or tradition. But I am not at all sure that that has ever been demonstrated.

Until we know more than we now do about the origins of materials now found in written form in the documents at hand, we cannot claim that they are traditions, in the ordinary sense of the word. We can only allege that they are stories or sayings now found in the documents at hand. These stories or sayings may in fact prove to be traditions. How so? They may be shown to have undergone a long process of handing on, from one generation to the next, <u>prior</u> to being written down in the document at hand. But we cannot impute the status of "tradition" to what is in fact only a story or a saying. We have to prove that the pre-history of the story or saying permits us to classify it in that other category, namely, a story of a saying that has been handed on for a long time prior to reaching written form in the document at hand.

Providing an example of how the "tradition"-theory of the multiplicity of versions demands attention to the thesis that an "original" "tradition" was handed on. For without the claim that a given version stands close(st) to an "original" "tradition," the point that a version falls into the classification of tradition is difficult to discern. That is to say, I do not see that we have gained very much if we claim that people have handed a story or saying on over a period of time, but if we do not <u>also</u> claim that one version of that "tradition" leads us closer to the "original" than some other. If alongside the theory of "tradition" we do not find a theory of "originality," perhaps even a claim of historicity made in behalf of the "original" "tradition," then the theory of tradition yields trivial observations. More important, the theory by itself never becomes susceptible to verification or falsification. We never know when we are wrong, therefore we cannot know that we are right. Making up a long "pre-history" of "tradition" back to an "original" version of the tradition therefore leads us deep into the imagination of the scholar who makes up the theory. It is a study of the contemporary imagination, that alone.

Accordingly, the allegation of "tradition" ordinarily bears in its wake the claim of "original." The claim of the language at hand is this: <u>something happened that has been put into permanent verbal formulas through oral formulation and then oral transmission and handed on for some time</u>. Then, if we have a number of versions of a given saying or story, these several versions permit us to speculate, as we move backward from the latest tradition to an earlier one and finally to the first, the "original(s)," about the character and wording even of the "original(s)" of the "tradition." In this framework we may speak of the original tradition (now no longer needing quotation-marks).

In order to deal with the present theory on how to interpret thrice-told tales, I wish to lay out the three versions of sayings assigned to lists of recurrent names, or, as these versions are conventionally called, the "chains of Pharisaic tradition." That is to say, in what follows we look for what is original to closely related, yet distinct, versions of a given list. We shall find that, when we have recovered what appears to be the original version of the tradition, hence, the original tradition, we have not gained very much. We know, in point of fact, little more than that there was, at some point, a list that people used for lining up sets of quite diverse sayings about topics in no way related to one another. That is the upshot of the theory at hand when brought to bear on the sources best suited to receive that theory.

We have three "chains of Pharisaic tradition," listing authorities of the party and assigning to them either moral apophthegms, purity decrees, or rulings on a minor aspect of the conduct of the sacrificial cult. These chains follow in probable order.

1. To Lay on Hands
A. Yose b. Yoezer says [on a Festival-day] not to lay [hands on the offering before it is slaughtered]. Yose b. Yohanan says to lay [hands].
B. Joshua b. Perahiah says not to lay [hands]. Nittai the Arbelite says to lay [hands].
C. Judah b. Tabbai says not to lay [hands]. Simeon b. Shetah says to lay [hands].
D. Shemaiah says to lay [hands]. Abtalion says not to lay [hands].
E. Hillel and Menahem did not differ, but Menahem went forth, and Shammai entered in.
F. Shammai says not to lay [hands]. Hillel says to lay [hands].
G. The former were <u>nasis</u>, and the later fathers of the court ('BWT BYUT DYN).

M. Hagigah 2:2

The opinions are in indirect discourse, "says to lay," "says not to lay." Normally "says" is followed by direct discourse. Someone has supplied the subscription (G) that the first-named were <u>nasis</u>, the second-named, heads of the court, considerations which do not figure in the body of the pericope and are irrelevant to its contents. But the pattern is

not exact; the first-named <u>always</u> should say, <u>not to lay on hands</u>. Yet while Yose b.
Yoezer, Joshua b. Perahiah, and Judah b. Tabbai, say <u>not</u> to do so, Shemaiah has the wrong
opinion for his position in the list. The little group at the end, Hillel-Menahem, then
Shammai-Hillel, is also difficult. Hillel-Menahem break the pattern; the lemma is a later
insertion. In fact, Hillel should say <u>not to lay on hands</u>, since he was supposed to have
been <u>nasi</u>. We have already seen a story on this very point, in which Hillel is represented
as following Shammai's practice.

Clearly, in the pericope before us Hillel is presumed to be <u>nasi</u>, despite the wrong
opinion. But if we drop the interpolation of Hillel-Menahem, we find what the form calls
for, merely: Shammai/Hillel: not to lay/lay, and that is surely the authentic reading
according to the foregoing pattern. Therefore the original list had Shammai as <u>nasi</u>, Hillel
as head of the court. The switch with Menahem (otherwise unknown) permits placing
Hillel first, therefore makes him <u>nasi</u>, according to the subscription, so it becomes
Hillel-Menahem-Shammai-Hillel. I cannot guess why Shemaiah's opinion has been
reversed.

In Tos. Hag., R. Meir provides a far better solution to the problem of making Hillel
<u>nasi</u> in traditions which originally have him as father of the court. Tos. Hag. 2:8 (ed.
Lieberman, p. 382-3, lines 40-44) is as follows:

> They differed only on the laying of hands.
>
> "They are five pairs. The three of the first pairs who said not to lay on
> hands, and the two of the last pairs who said to lay on hands were <u>nasis</u>. The
> second ones [mentioned] were heads of the court," so R. Meir.
>
> R. Judah said, "Simeon b. Shetah [was] <u>nasi</u>. Judah b. Tabbai [was] head
> of the court."

Meir thus has five pairs:

1. <u>Nasi</u> (not to lay)   + head of court (to lay)
2. <u>Nasi</u> (not to lay)   + head of court (to lay)
3. <u>Nasi</u> (not to lay)   + head of court (to lay)
4. <u>Nasi</u> (to lay)   + head of court (not to lay)
5. <u>Nasi</u> (to lay)   + head of court (not to lay)

Meir's list is the same as M. Hag. 2:2 as far as Shemaiah and Abtalion. He presumably had
no mention of Hillel-Menahem, for that would have made Hillel-Shammai a <u>sixth</u> pair.
But for the last pair he had a "to lay"-Nasi in first place. Was it Shammai or Hillel?
Probably Hillel, since the 'not to lay"/"to lay" antithesis is primary to the tradition, and
there seems no strong reason for changing the attributions. So we have two forms of the
list, one which can be reconstructed from M. Hag. 2:2, the other from Meir's report. They
agree for the first four pairs; for the first, the form behind M. Hag. 2:2 had <u>Shammai not,</u>
<u>Hillel to;</u> while Meir had <u>Hillel to, Shammai not.</u> Meir's tradition can be explained as a
secondary development from the other, motivated by the desire of the Hillelites to
represent Hillel as head of the government, <u>nasi</u>. What was done to the M. Hag. tradition

by inserting the Hillel-Menahem pair before Shammai and Hillel was done in Meir's
tradition by simply reversing the customary order and putting Hillel before Shammai.
This is neat and may be correct, but it leaves us with a second, unanswered problem: who
was Menahem and how did he get in? The possibility that the last of Meir's pairs may
have been, Hillel said to lay, menahem said no to lay, and there may have been no
reference at all to Shammai -- which would be understandable if we had an old list from
the House of Hillel -- cannot be wholly excluded. In that event Meir's list would be older
and M. Hag. would represent a post-70 revision, when the Shammaites and the Hillelites,
for survival's sake, combined their forces, the terms of the compromise (here) being that
Shammai's name would have precedence, but the law would in general follow Hillel.

Judah [b. Ilai] differs only with reference to Judah b. Tabbai and Simeon b. Shetah.
The latter, he says, was nasi.

The list of M. Hag., excluding Menahem and the subscription, could not have been
shaped later than the time of Meir and Judah, since both refer to it. Judah the Patriarch
follows Meir, therefore has a nasi Yose b. Yoezer, Joshua, Judah, Shemaiah, and Hillel.
Since he thought he descended from Hillel and referred to the Bene Bathyrans' giving up
their position to Hillel and making him nasi, it was natural to explain matters as he did in
the subscription. But the subscription in M. Hag. 2:2 cannot come before Meir-Judah, who
do not cite it verbatim. It looks like Judah the Patriarch's summary of Meir's comment.

2.   Decrees

DTNY':

1.   Yose b. Yoezer of Seredah and Yose b. Yohanan of Jerusalem decreed (GZR) [the
      capacity to receive] uncleanness upon the land of the people and on glassware.

2.   Simeon b. Shetah obtained (TQN) a marriage-contract for the wife and decreed
      (GZR) [the capacity to receive] uncleanness upon metal utensils.

3.   Shammai and Hillel decreed (GZR) uncleanness on hands.

                              (B. Shab. 14b)

Did not R. Zeira b. Abuna in the name of R. Jeremiah say, "Yosef b. Yoezer of
Seredah and Yose b. Yohanan of Jerusalem decreed uncleanness upon the land of the
peoples and upon glass utensils."

R. Yonah [Var.: Yuda] said, "Rabbi Judah b. Tabbai."

R. Yose said, "Rabbi Judah b. Tabbai and Simeon b. Shetah decreed uncleanness on
metal utensils.

"Hillel and Shammai decreed concerning the cleanness of the hands."

                  Y. Shab. 1:4 (= Y. Pes. 1:6, Y. Ket. 8:11)

The Babylonian beraita is a list of decrees. I assume Simeon b. Shetah's saying has
been contaminated by the reference to the ordinance (TQN) about the marriage-contract,
missing in y., which is out of place here, for all are decrees and concern uncleanness.
Judah b. Tabbai is absent -- thus following Judah b. Ilai -- and the Palestinian version

supplies his name, making the list Yose + Yose, _Judah_ + Simeon, and Hillel + Shammai, in all three instances with the _nasi_ first, hence following Meir in Tos. Hag., and (of course) placing Hillel in the nasi's position. The absence of Joshua b. Perahiah-Nittai the Arbelite is curious. The addition of the places of origin of the Yose's suggests that this might come after M. Hag., so I should also have expected the inclusion of the absent masters. Perhaps no one had traditions on uncleanness-decrees to attribute to the men. That guess depends upon the presumption that without considerable motivation people did not make up what they did not have. But often they did, as we have observed time and again.

The representation of Shammai as _nasi_, Hillel second to him, is congruent to the stories of the (temporary) predominance of the House of Shammai and of the (later) rise of the House of Hillel to power. It also explains why the Houses-form nearly always puts the Shammaite House ahead of the Hillelite one, in conformity with the order of M. Hag. The later masters, coming long after the Hillelite hegemony had been well established by the patriarchate, appropriately doctored the earlier materials in the ways that have become evident.

This explanation however takes for granted two allegations of the later Tannaim, first, that Yohanan b. Zakkai took over from Shammai and Hillel and was Hillel's heir; second, that the Yavnean patriarch Gamaliel was descended from Hillel. But the allegation that Yohanan b. Zakkai was Hillel's continuator first occurs in M. Avot, which, as we shall see, comes later than the M. Hag.-chain. No Tannaitic or early Amoraic authority refers to Yohanan b. Zakkai as Hillel's disciple, and it is primarily in the highly developed traditions of ARN that Yohanan's discipleship to Hillel plays a considerable role. The _beraitot_ of b. Suk. = b. B.B., which make something of the fact, are apt to be later than, and based upon, Avot, therefore do not change matters.

More strikingly still, in all the Gamaliel-traditions -- pertaining either to the first or the second one -- we find not the slightest allusion to the familial relationship between Gamaliel and Hillel. To the contrary, Gamaliel II-materials persistently allege that Simeon b. Gamaliel I followed Shammaite rules, certainly an extraordinary state of affairs for the "grandson" (or great-grandson) of Hillel himself. It is moreover remarkable that Simeon b. Gamaliel and Gamaliel I never occur in he Houses-materials. The heirs of Hillel (Yohanan b. Zakkai, Gamaliel) and the House of Hillel on the face of it have nothing whatever to do with one another. It may therefore be anachronistic to suppose that the Hillelites predominated _because_ Yohanan b. Zakkai and Gamaliel II were the greatest student and the great-grandson of Hillel, respectively. It looks as if things were the other way around. They were given a relationship to Hillel because they came to power at a point at which the Hillelate House predominated, and the allegation that both were Hillelites was the condition of their leadership at Yavneh. Strikingly, while that allegation later was important, no one took the trouble to invent stories in which either authority ever cited "my master" or "my father" Hillel. As I said, no named authority from Hillel to Yavneh ever quotes Hillel. But the predominance of Hillelites at Yavneh is very well attested and may be regarded as an axiom. Nothing in the Tannaitic stratum of Yohanan b. Zakkai-materials places him into relationship with either the House of

Shammai or the House of Hillel. Yohanan cites "my teachers" back to Moses, but never
mentions Hillel (M. Yad. 4:3). This seems to me probative that the circles of Yohanan's
immediate disciples had no traditions relating Yohanan to Hillel. Similarly, Gamaliel II
repeatedly is given references to "the house of father," meaning Simeon b. Gamaliel I, but
none to Hillel, directly or inferentially.

3. Moral Apophthegms

1. A. Moses received the Torah from Sinai and handed it on to Joshua, Joshua to the
       Elders, the Elders to the Prophets; and the Prophets handed it on to the men of
       the Great Assembly (KNST).
   B. They said three things, "Be deliberate in judgment, raise up many disciples,
       and make a fence around the Torah."

2. Simeon the Just was of the remnants of the Great Assembly. He used to say, "On
   three things the world stands: on the Torah, on the [Temple-] service, and on deeds
   of loving kindness."

3. Antigonus of Sokho received from Simeon the Just. He used to say, "Be not like
   slaves that minister to the master for the sake of receiving a reward, but be like
   slaves that minister to the master not for the sake of receiving a reward; and let the
   fear of heaven be upon you."

4. Yose b. Yoezer of Seredah and Yose b. Yohanan of Jerusalem received from them
   [sic].
   Yose b. Yoezer says, "Let your house be a meeting-house for the Sages, and sit amid
   the dust of their feet, and thirstily drink in their words."

5. A. Yose b. Yohanan of Jerusalem says, "Let your house be opened wide; and let
       the needy be members of your house; and do not talk much with a woman."
   B. They said this of a man's own wife: how much more of his fellow's wife!
       Hence the Sages have said, "He that talks much with women brings evil upon
       himself, and neglects the study of the Law, and at the end he inherits
       Gehenna."

6. Joshua b. Perahiah and Nittai the Arbelite received from them.
   Joshua b. Perahiah says, "Make for yourself a master (RB), and get a fellow (HBR)
   [-disciple]; and judge any man with the balance in his favor."

7. Nittai the Arbelite says, "Keep far from an evil neighbor, and do not consort with a
   wicked neighbor, and do not despair of retribution."

8. Judah b. Tabbai and Simeon b. Shetah received from them. Judah b. Tabbai says,
   "Make not yourself like them that would influence the judges; and when the suitors
   stand before you, let them be in your eyes as wicked men; and when they have
   departed from before you, let them be in your eyes as innocent, as soon as they have
   accepted the judgment."

9. Simeon b. Shetah says, "Abundantly examine the witnesses; and be cautious in your
   words, lest from them they learn to swear falsely."

10. Shemaiah and Avtalion received from them. Shemaiah says, "Love work; and hate
    mastery (RBNWT), and seek not acquaintance with the ruling power (RSWT)."

11.   Avtalion says, "Sages, give heed to your words, lest you incur the penalty of exile, and be exulted to a place of evil waters, and the disciples that come after you drink and die, and the name of Heaven be profaned."

12.   Hillel and Shammai received from them.

Hillel says, "Be of the disciples of Aaron, loving peace, and pursuing peace, loving mankind, and bringing them near to the Torah."

13.   He used to say, "<u>A name made great is a name destroyed, and he that increases not decreases, and he that learns not is worthy of death, and he that makes worldly use of the crown perishes.</u>"

14.   He used to say, "If I am not for myself who is for me? And being for mine own self, what am I? And if not now, when?"

15.   Shammai says, "Make your [study of] Torah [a] fixed [habit]. say little and do much. And receive all men with a cheerful countenance."

16.   Rabban Gamaliel says, "Make for yourself a master (RB) [=Joshua b. Perahiah's saying, above]; and keep distant from doubt; and do not tithe by guesswork."

17.   Simeon his son says, "All my days I have grown up among the sages, and I have found nothing better for the person (GWP) than silence; and the expounding is not the principle, but the doing; and he that multiplies words occasions sin."

18.   Rabban Simeon b. Gamaliel says, "On three things the world stands: on truth, on judgment, and on peace, as it is written, <u>Execute the judgment of truth and peace</u> (Zech. 8:16)."

M. Avot. 1:1-18

The form from no. 4 to no. 12 is fixed: the names of the two who received the Torah from the foregoing, then apophthegms assigned to each, in order. The apophthegms are always triplicates; each <u>says</u> ('WMR) three things.

The list is heavily glossed. In no. 5, for example, we are given a <u>qal vehomer</u>, which then produces a saying of the sages. In no. 8, <u>as soon as they have accepted</u> makes specific what has already been presupposed by <u>when they have departed</u>. Its purpose is to rule out the possible objection, "What if they have not accepted the judgment?" -- a typical sort of Talmudic quibble. Avtalion's saying is not a triplicate, but the three evil consequences make up for the absence of three separate sayings. No. 3 is expanded by the affirmative revision and the gloss, thus three. Nos. 13 and 14 are added to Hillel's saying, not a gloss but a considerable interpolation of materials, some in Aramaic, occurring elsewhere. Now it is <u>used to say</u> (HYH 'WMR) as in nos. 2-3.

Strikingly, with Hillel and Shammai the pairs cease. Also Gamaliel, standing alone, is not said to "receive" from Hillel/Shammai, nor Simeon from Gamaliel. Gamaliel's saying follows the earlier form. Simeon's does not, for it is glossed by <u>all my days ... I have found</u>, making an apophthegm, "There is naught better" into an autobiographical comment. But the rest of the saying conforms to the earlier pattern. Then in no. 18, Simeon <u>his son</u> becomes <u>Rabban</u> Simeon b. <u>Gamaliel</u> and is given a statement incongruent to the foregoing form. That saying is a counterpart of Simeon the Just's, though the specification of the "three things" changes, and is glossed with a Scriptural proof-text. What is striking is the persistence of the "three things" form in the sayings that come in-between. No. 18 has been tacked on to the foregoing list to close with a parallel to no. 2.

Simeon the Just's saying is parallel to Simeon b. Gamaliel's, which clearly represents a post-135 revision of no. 2: the Torah now is truth, a philosophizing tendency; the temple service is now replaced by justice; and deeds of lovingkindness are replaced by peace. That this conclusion balances no. 2, and not the saying in no. 1, strongly suggests that no. 2 was originally the first saying in the list, and that the saying in no. 1 is a later addition, putting at the head of the whole list the fundamental principles of the rabbinic academy as a social form.

But the fact that no. 18 was added to balance no. 2 raises the problem about no. 2 itself: Was it an integral part of the list? We saw that the fixed form characteristic of the list ("A + B received from them; A said [three sayings]; B said [three sayings]") begins only with no. 4. Thus on formal grounds there are strong reasons for thinking that nos. 2 and 3 were secondary accretions, and since the rabbinic traditions had no substantial legal materials from Simeon the Just and Antigonus -- indeed, ignored Antigonus and treated Simeon primarily through legends -- the case is clear. The original list began just as the rabbinic legal tradition began: with the two Yose's. The appeal to Simeon the Just, perhaps known from Ben Sira, was motivated by the desire to attach this legal tradition to the last great member of the legitimate Jerusalem priesthood before its fall. Simeon's function is therefore the same as that of Moses etc., -- he is part of the biblical (and Ben Sira) stemma of the tradition of the law. Antigonus as put in to bridge the temporal gap between Simeon and the Yose's -- a whole century! Whence did they get him? We have no idea.

Another mystery is the beginning of no. 4: the two Yose's received from them, when the solitary Antigonus has preceded them. This probably is confirmation of our conjecture that Simeon and Antigonus have been added. The original referent of them will have been "the men of the great synagogue" -- a single mythologumenon which bridged the gap from the prophets to the Pharisees. The original list was thus 1A, 4, 5A, 6, 7, 8, 9, 10, 11, 12, and 15. This elegant structure was broken to insert Simeon and thus claim connection with the last of the legitimate priesthood, and also to make the representation that the priesthood put the law ahead of the Temple service.

After no. 18, M. Avot 2 begins with the yet later additions from the patriarch's circle, Rabbi, and Rabban Gamaliel III (M. Avot 2:1, 2:2ff), and then a collection of sayings of Hillel, purported ancestor of the patriarchal house, and then in Avot 2:8 comes an earlier addition to the list: Rabban Yohanan b. Zakkai received [the Torah] from Hillel and Shammai. This, which does have the form of the earlier entries, clearly is what has been displaced by the intervening (inserted) patriarchal material. The pre-70 list was therefore expanded by his pupils before it was taken over by the patriarchate. From the material following M. Avot. 2:8 (Yohanan's pupils and their sayings) we can see how it was developed in his school, by contrast to the patriarchal development. The Mishnah combines the two traditions.

The names on the lists compare as follows

M.Hag. 2:2	B. Shab. 14b = y.Shab. 1:4	M. Avot 1:1 1-18
		Moses
		Joshua
		Elders
		Prophets
		Men of the Great Synagogue
		Simeon the Just
		Antigonus of Sokho

Yose b. Yoezer	Yose b. Yoezer of Seredah	Yose b. Yoezer of Seredah
Yose b. Yohanan	Yose b. Yohanan of Jerusalem	Yose b. Yohanan of Jerusalem
Joshua b. Perahiah		Joshua b. Perahiah
Nittai the Arbelite		Nittai the Arbelite
Judah b. Tabbai	[y.: Judah b. Tabbai	Judah b. Tabbai
Simeon b. Shetah	and] Simeon b. Shetah	Simeon b. Shetah
Shemaiah		Shemaiah
Avtalion		Avtalion
Hillel-Menahem	Shammai	Hillel
Shammai-Hillel	Hillel	Shammai
	[y.: Hillel and Shammai]	

		Gamaliel [omits: received]
		Simeon b. Gamaliel [omits: received]

[2.8: Yohanan b. Zakkai
received from Hillel and
Shammai]

The second names in the first two pairs, Yose b. Yohanan and Nittai the Arbelite,
elsewhere are given no independent sayings whatever. They occur only in the
context of the first-mentioned names, Yose b. Yoezer and Joshua b. Perahiah.
Further, Shemaiah and Avtalion are rarely separated at all, but, except in Avot,
normally appear as a pair, with remarkably few independent lemmas attributed to
either the one or the other. They are given common ancestry. The first two Yose's
are not supplied with places of origin in M. Hag.

M. Avot corresponds to M. Hag. where the two coincide, except in the
additions of the places of origin of Yose's, and in the reversal of the order to
Hillel-Shammai, making Hillel nasi; the subscription of M. Hag. serves the same
purpose. The Babylonian version of the cleanness-decree lists does not conform.

The names tacked on to the Avot-list obviously serve to complete the story
back to Moses, on the one side, and to A.D. 170, on the other. Gamaliel is made the
heir of Hillel's Torah. The Simeon mentioned in the beraita in b. Shab. 15a is
ignored; perhaps the compiler of the Avot-list did not know that beraita.

Since no extant materials have either Simeon b. Gamaliel or Gamaliel I
referring to Hillel, we may suppose that the claim of Hillel as an ancestor by the
patriarchate came some time after the destruction of the Temple. My guess is that
it was first alleged quite a long time later one. Judah the Patriarch's circle
probably is responsible for the additions of Gamaliel and Simeon b. Gamaliel to the
Avot list. Since that same circle also produced the genealogy linking Hillel to David
-- presumably because the Babylonian exilarch did the same -- the link between
Gamaliel I and Hillel may have come some time before Judah the Patriarch, who is
the first patriarch to refer to Hillel as his ancestor. The link is to be traced to the
point at which the patriarchate made peace with the growing predominance of the
Hillelite House, some time soon after the destruction of the Temple. Before then
the Shammaites apparently predominated within Pharisaism, and Simeon b. Gamaliel
probably was one of them, which accounts for the suppression of virtually all of his
legal traditions. The first point at which Hillelite claim would have served the
patriarchate therefore was the time of Gamaliel II. But, since Gamaliel II is
represented as following Shammaite law (e.g. b. Yev. 15b), makes no reference to
Hillel, plays no role in the Hillel-pericopae or in Hillel's House's materials, as I said,
and tells how his father Simeon followed Shammaite rules, the Hillelite ancestry for
the patriarchate founded by Gamaliel II may not have been established until ca. 150,
by which time it seems to be settled. That is the point at which Meir had to revise
the form of the earlier list to make Hillel nasi.

Yose b. Halafta, Meir's contemporary, knew nothing about b. Shab. 14b, and
said the decree about the uncleanness of glassware and the land of the people in fact

was in force (with no authority given) eighty years before the destruction of the
Temple. The masters certainly recognized that the two Yose's long antedated Hillel
and Shammai. Therefore Yose b. Halafta's tradition was separate from, and
contradicted, b. Shab. He presumably knew no other. It therefore may be that that
beraita comes well after ca. 150, as the names of Palestinian Talmud's authorities
suggest.

4. Conclusion

The "original" "tradition" consisted of the following names:

1.   Yose b. Yoezer
    2.   Yose b. Yohanan
3.   Joshua b. Perahiah
    4.   Nittai the Arbelite
5.   Judah b. Tabai
    6.   Simeon b. Shetah
7.   Shemaiah
    +
8.   Avtalion
9.   Shammai
    10.   Hillel
11.   Yohanan b. Zakkai
12.   Yohanan's disciples
    Replaced by
13.   Gamaliel
14.   Simeon b. Gamaliel

Of the foregoing, nos. 2 and 4 exist in the traditions only in association with
nos. 1 and 3, nos. 7 and 8 are always connected. As we shall see, furthermore, the
relationships between nos. 5 and 6 are extremely complex, and it looks as if separate
traditions of the two masters may have been put together for a post facto explanation of the union of two originally unrelated circles of disciples. To revert to the
point at which we began, if we now have the "original" "tradition," it surely does not
amount to much. More important, the theory of the "original" "tradition" proves
irrelevant to most of the data at hand. So if the theory is right, then, so what? And
the answer is, so nothing.

CHAPTER FIFTEEN
INCREMENTAL HISTORY
"WHEN HE WAS A STUDENT ... AND WHEN HE GREW UP ..."

Sages of ancient times recognized that sayings and stories appeared in diverse versions. They too proposed explanations of how a given saying or story could come down in more than a single statement. The principal approach to the question posited that each detail represented a different stage in the history of the story, or of the life of its hero in particular, with one version characteristic of one such stage, and another version attesting to a different, and later one. So the successive versions of a saying or story supply a kind of incremental history. How so? Each version tells something about concrete events and real lives (biographies) that earlier versions did not reveal.

The classic Talmudic expression of the incremental theory takes up a passage of the Mishnah in which Rabban Yohanan ben Zakkai is called merely "Ben Zakkai:"

The precedent is as follows: Ben Zakkai examined a witness as to the character of the stalks of figs [under which an incident now subject to court procedure was alleged to have taken place].

Mishnah Sanhedrin 5:2B

As we shall now see, at paragraph N in the following talmudic analysis, exactly the same story is reported, on Tannaite authority. Now Rabban Yohanan ben Zakkai is alleged to have made exactly the same ruling, in exactly the same case. The item is worded in the same way except for the more fitting title. Then, at P-Q, the two versions are readily explained as facts of history. The one of Ben Zakkai was framed when he was a mere disciple. When, later on, he had become a recognized sage, the story was told to take account of that fact. So the theory I call "incremental history" is simple: each story related to, because it derives from, historical moments in a linear progression. The Talmudic passage is as follows:

IX.
A. Who is this "Ben Zakkai"?
B. If we should proposed that it is R. Yohanan ben Zakkai, did he ever sit in a sanhedrin [that tried a murder case]?
C. And has it not been taught on Tannaite authority:
D. The lifetime of R. Yohanan ben Zakkai was a hundred and twenty years. For forty years he engaged in trade, for forty years he studied [Torah], and for forty years he taught.
E. And it has been taught on Tannaite authority: Forty years before the destruction of the Temple the sanhedrin went into exile and conducted its sessions in Hanut.

F.   And said R. Isaac bar Abodimi, "That is to say that the sanhedrin did not judge cases involving penalties."

G.   Do you think it was cases involving penalties? [Such cases were not limited to the sanhedrin but could be tried anywhere in the Land of Israel.]

H.   Rather, the sanhedrin did not try capital cases.

I.   And we have learned in the Mishnah:

J.   After the destruction of the house of the sanctuary, Rabban Yohanan b. Zakkai ordained ... [M. R.H. 4:1]. [So the final forty years encompassed the period after the destruction of the Temple, and Yohanan could not, therefore, have served on a sanhedrin that tried capital cases.]

K.   Accordingly, at hand is some other Ben Zakkai [than Yohanan b. Zakkai].

L.   That conclusion, moreover, is reasonable, for if you think that it is Rabban Yohanan ben Zakkai, would Rabbi [in the Mishnah-passage] have called him merely, "Ben Zakkai"? [Not very likely.]

M.   And lo, it has been taught on Tannaite authority:

N.   There is the precedent that Rabban Yohanan ben Zakkai conducted an interrogation about the stalks on the figs [so surely this is the same figure as at M. 5:2B].

O.   But [at the time at which the incident took place, capital cases were tried by the sanhedrin and] he was a disciple in session before his master. He said something, and the others found his reasoning persuasive, [41B] so they adopted [the ruling] in his name.

P.   When he was studying Torah, therefore, he was called Ben Zakkai, as a disciple in session before his master, but when he [later on] taught, he was called Rabban Yohanan ben Zakkai.

Q.   When, therefore, he is referred to as Ben Zakkai, it is on account of his being a beginning [student] and when he is called Rabban Yohanan b. Zakkai, it is on account of his status later on.

The relevance of the Talmudic passage is simple, as I shall now explain.

Modernist scholars have claimed to explain diverse versions of a single saying or story by much the same thesis as we see before us. That is to say, they alleged that they know why a given detail is added here, dropped there, changed in the third place, built up and augmented in the fourth, and on and on. Accordingly, the modern, critical scholars accomplish a kind of incremental history. This is the history of what happened to account for changes in versions of a story, based on a theory of what might have impelled an author to add or revise a given detail. Indeed, practitioners of the incremental approach have not hesitated to declare that they know an entire history for which the text at hand supplies no evidence whatsoever. They then refer to this (entirely undocumented) history in order to explain shifts and changes in versions of a story.

The single best example of the fantasy at hand is supplied by David J. Halperin, The Merkabah in Rabbinic Literature (New Haven, 1980: American Oriental Series 62). Halperin refers to the Merkavah-materials, with which we made our acquaintance in

Chapter One. He posits that, prior to the first written version there was an entire cycle of such stories ("presumably oral"!). He knows that one of these stories had a narrative framework, then lost a miraculous element, then got that miracle reinserted later on. This literary history, claiming to explain shifts and changes in the sequence of stories we saw earlier, derives from not a shred of evidence of any kind. There is no version of these stories at all. The author just made it up and wrote it down, then the American Oriental Society printed it as "scholarship." True, as we shall note, Halperin introduces appropriate qualifications and caveats. But he pays little attention to them; they are mainly formalities. Here is how he states his conclusions (pp. 138-9):

1. I postulate the following development for the merkabah tradition involving R. Johanan b. Zakkai: (1) A cycle of merkabah stories, presumably oral, recounted the miracles that accompanied the expositions of one or another of R. Johanan's disciples; the stories of this cycle contained little beside the miracles. (This stage is purely hypothetical, and is not attested by any literary source.) (2) One of these stories, which involved R. Eleazar b. Arakh, was given a narrative framework, which suggested that R. Eleazar exemplified the "scholar" of M. Hag. 2:1 (Mek. Rashbi). (3) The miraculous element was "censored" from the story of R. Eleazar, possibly by the compiler of the mystical collection (Tosefta). (4) Miraculous details were reinserted, and stories of other disciples added, on the basis of the old merkabah stories (PT, BT)....

3. If my hypothesis is correct, the merkabah tradition is rooted in a cycle of miraculous legends. Some historical reality may hide behind these legends, but it is nearly inaccessible. Instead of trying to recover it, we should focus on what the legends can teach us about (maaseh) merkabah and the image of those reported to have been expert in it.

Halperin's exposition of his own theories omits all reference to whatever he holds as a fundamental thesis on the character of the literature and its formation, if any. Yet even on the surface, it is clear, he proposes to make up explanations for diverse versions of the Merkavah-story. Each detail has its day. None is spared the ravages of Halperin's imaginative reconstruction of its individual life-history. Everything means something somewhere -- and to Halperin it does not matter where. It follows that the theory of "incremental history," assigning a particular event or motive or other explanation for each change in a story as it moves from document to document finds exemplification in Halperin's treatment of the Merkavah-story.

A systematic picture of what Halperin has done and why it is founded on false premises (or on no premises other than an undisciplined imagination) derives from William Scott Green's review of Halperin's book.

In his review (the Second Century, 1983, 3:113-115) Green observes:

> For reasons never specified, Halperin tends to construe each literary unit,
> each manuscript variant, and each textual version as a discrete historical
> moment. he then constructs his history by arranging these textual moments
> into chronological sequence. By adopting this strategy, Halperin forces
> himself into the grueling exercise of determining the relative dates of
> decontextualized literary segments. Much is at stake in these demonstrations;
> the very possibility of Halperin's history depends on their rigor and cogency.
> Halperin uses a wide range of criteria to date his materials, and he sometimes
> deploys these inconsistently. That is, he established his chronologies on the
> basis of the differences among versions of a passage. But the variables he
> deems decisive are not systematically applied. Rather, they seem to shift
> from case to case. This sort of unevenness undermines Halperin's demon-
> strations of chronology and makes at least some of them appear arbitrary.
> The problems of particular chronologies aside, Halperin's method limits the
> kind of history of rabbinic, merkabah speculation he can write. His catenae of
> textual events result in schematic accounts that flip and flop, sparse
> chronicles of unexpected reversals and inversions in which discrete passages
> undergo marked, sometimes radical shifts of meaning. He argues, for
> instance, that the Mishnaic rule that the merkabah may not be expounded "by
> an individual [variant: to an individual], unless he is a scholar, understanding
> on his own" (M. Hagigah 2:1) had three distinct meanings before the time of
> Tosefta's redaction (ca. A.D. 250). When the passage circulated indepen-
> dently, it allowed the sage, but not the disciple, "to undertake on his own an
> exegesis of Ezekiel's vision" (p. 35). When it was redacted into the Mishnah
> and incorporated into a list of other biblical passages whose exposition is
> restricted, "the effect was to reverse the other biblical passages whose
> exposition is restricted, "the effect was to reverse the meaning of the
> merkabah ruling; solitary study of the merkabah was no longer the object of
> the restriction, but a concession granted to certain exceptional individuals" (p.
> 36). Still later, the meaning of the rule was changed again to make it "refer to
> instruction" (p. 36), an alteration reflected in the variant reading. This final
> meaning is apparent in a story about Yohanan b. Zakkai and Eleazar b. Arakh
> at T. Hagigah 2:1, which, ironically, preserves the earliest version of the
> Mishnaic rule.

This kind of lean and linear history disappoints because it does not account for
the changes it describes. Even if Halperin's textual sequences are correct,
they leave too much unexplained. For instance, to whom within rabbinism
were these changes important? Did the different meanings supersede one
another or exist simultaneously? Are these changes literary, or do they

reflect deeper theological, religious, and social diversions within rabbinism? Are such changes, particularly the reversal of meaning, accidental or deliberate, the result of misunderstanding or of manipulation? Without some theory of rabbinic culture and society, of textual transmission and tradition, and of literary tendencies, Halperin's textual sequences lead nowhere. They are merely chronologies masquerading as history.

In singling Halperin out, my intent is only to show what people are doing now. I do not want anyone to suppose that I have taken a particularly weak example of an otherwise vital theory. On the contrary, Halperin presents us with as capable an exercise of the incremental-historical theory as is in print -- alas. For it seems he is talking to himself, in the privacy of his study. He clearly is not engaging in reasoned arguments with the generality of interested participants in the inquiry. Only by that theory can I explain how anyone can make up a "cycle" of Merkavah-stories ("presumably oral"), tell us what was in them, then what was removed from them -- and only then relate the whole to the actual sources at hand. The theory that details in successive versions of a saying or story bears historical meanings deserves better than it has gotten to date.

The approach that seeks to account for shifts and changes by reference to the interests of later authors, tradents, and redactors, remains entirely open. Indeed, in due course we may look forward to the rehabilitation of the theory at hand. My criticism, like Green's, is that, so far as Halperin exemplifies the theory, he provides yet another instance of the dreary approach of made-up explanations, never subjected to tests of falsification or validation. That approach, suitable for talmudic exegesis, does not serve for historical and literary work in our day. While both the theory that "he often used to say ..." and the claim that there is an "original" "tradition," promise little for the future, the one at hand awaits rigorous attention.

PART FOUR

CONCLUSION

CHAPTER SIXTEEN
A DOCUMENTARY-HISTORICAL THEORY

The reader will not find surprising the allegation that the authors of later documents in the canon of Judaism in a fairly consistent way fill holes in stories and sayings received from earlier ones. When, therefore, we wish to explain why details are added or dropped, the first appeal will carry us to the matter of rhetoric. We ask whether we are able to explain why a detail makes a first appearance by asking about the relative relationship of the document in which it surfaces to other documents in which it is absent. If we can show that the document bearing the fresh fact comes later in the formation of the canon than the one lacking it, we may appeal first of all to the claim that the later authors' sense of rhetoric, their larger aesthetic theory, precipitated their making up and including that detail. That hypothesis will gain substantial credibility if we can show that, in general, authors of the document at hand did pretty much the same thing with whatever they received.

Yet the theory at hand, which I call the documentary theory, marks the beginning, not the ending, of the matter. For aesthetics, including rhetoric, in the system at hand brings to expression the fundamental and generative character of the system as a whole. Aesthetics constitutes a cultural indicator and relates in a contingent way to the culture -- in this case, the textual community -- at hand. To invoke a theory of aesthetics by itself as explanation of why rhetoric takes one form rather than some other simply is to beg the question. Why so? Because in a truly integrated community of culture, such as the canon of Judaism attests to the sages of late antiquity, each detail addresses the whole. Each one in some small way expresses the character of the entire system. The sages' own convictions about the utter harmony of the hole, the congruity of law to theology, of meal-time to bed-time and of conduct in the toilet to behavior in the synagogue, reenforce the claim at hand. Indeed these commonplace allegations bring it to explicit expression. It must follow that, when we appeal to a rhetorical explanation for the facts at hand and therefore treat the matter as an essentially literary problem, we have only succeeded in restating the question, not resolving it. Aesthetics, including rhetoric, adds up to little more than making something out of interesting arrangements of words into patterns. By itself it constitutes a formalist inquiry into formalism, a quest for trivial explanations of small things.

The fact that later sages rewrote in their own way what earlier sages had handed on to them looms as an enormous presence in the interpretation of the formative age of Judaism. As I said at the end of Chapter One, the sages at hand surely do not conform to the definition of traditionalism ordinarily imputed to their culture. For while they faithfully handed on what they had received, it never was never intact, if in their view it always was unimpaired. Why so? Because they saw for themselves a role in the process of formation of what would be "the tradition." That role proved inventive, therefore creative. It must follow that the facts of rhetorical preference and the configuration of a larger sense of aesthetics in important ways convey definitive traits of the system at hand. But describing and analyzing those traits, interpreting them in context for what they reveal about the larger system -- these labors only now begin.

What I have done here is to dismiss some silly notions and to ask in an urgent way for the reconsideration of the significance of facts hitherto explained away and never explained. The task accomplished here proved pressing because the old modes of thought -- "He often used to say...," "When he was a student..., and when he grew up...," not to mention the theory of an "original" "tradition" -- continue to flourish, and not only in stagnant backwaters of the eastern Mediterranean.

Still more ominous, the theory of a linear development of a single "tradition," leading to the whole and harmonious completion in the Bavli, itself obscures far more than it illuminates. For the documents at hand seen one by one exhibit only limited harmony and cogency. It must follow that the documents first have to testify to their own context and setting. Only then can they tell us anything about the relationships between each of them and the next and among them all. To such an exercise the theory of a single and linear movement from one place to the next presents a barrier. To the contrary, I at the outset insisted that the Bavli stands at the end only to make a simple point. It is that the beginning of all inquiry into the meanings of the diversity of versions of a given saying or story carries us to traits of documents, what they generally do, how they ordinarily hand on what they have received. Aesthetic theory communicates inner concerns, points of tension, generative and definitive characteristics, of the authors of the documents, who write in one way, not in another. In their aesthetic choices, these authors express the deepest convictions of their system -- their culture, their textual community and its context. So, as I cannot overemphasize, aesthetics marks the beginning. But aesthetics does supply an indicator and present a starting-point.

To move forward, the theory I have called "incremental history" fails not because it lacks merit, but because it lacks successful exemplars. If we are to move on, the route must carry us not from one detail to the next, but to a height affording a perspective overall. Once we have a theory of how to proceed and a thesis worth testing, then, but only then, we move to the details, from large to small, in proper and proportionate succession. Beginning from the outside and systematically working our way within, we first seek large and definitive traits. These then will tell us what to discern in the small field of an individual story.

The incremental-historical theory then undergoes an appropriately rigorous exercise of falsification. How so? We must ask whether details conform to the main point. The alternative is that we make things up as we go along, text by text and detail by detail like Halperin. But a useful theory will prove its worth if we are able to explain and even predict the course of matters in a consistent and cogent way. The ultimately useless result of Halperin's work, surveyed just now, derives not from the rather private and subjective character of the results, his meditations on this and that. Even though it is easy to dismiss as mere subjectivity Halperin's power of making up version after version of a tradition no one has ever seen, then appealing to hypothetical version A to explain what is lost in imaginary version C, that is not the main point. It is the methodological inconsistency, the made-up character of the whole approach, not merely the manufactured quality of the individual parts that requires us to dismiss Haplerin's work as hopeless. A useful and plausible theory works wholesale, not retail. It cannot come tailor-made but has to come right off the plain pipe rack, so to speak. Halperin's exemplification of all that can go wrong with the incremental theory therefore should not lead to the dismissal of the theory. What we have to do is more thoughtfully consider how to proceed from the documentary facts, awaiting discovery, to the explanation of the documents' preferences, overall, and then also to details of a given story (such as the Merkavah-one), in proper sequence.

Fifteen years ago I attempted such a program in Development of a Legend. Studies on the Traditions Concerning Yohanan ben Zakkai, (Leiden, 1970). What I proposed to do was explain why a story appeared with one set of details in one document, and with a different set of details in another. I used two methods. First, I compared versions of the same story as they appeared in successive texts. Second. I asked about the larger tendencies of the framers of the texts, viewed one by one. So the two approaches I advocate here to the problem of sorting out and making sense of diverse versions of a saying or a story -- documentary, then incremental-historical -- find ample illustration in Development of a Legend. The main point is that I appealed to the then-established facts that one document came from one school among the talmudic sages, another and parallel document from a different school. I took the view that traits (at that time) pretty well known to characterize one school might also guide me to explain why that same school would tell a story in one way and not in some other. This I did for the entire corpus of sayings and stories concerning Yohanan ben Zakkai.

The book failed for a host of reasons. In that naive period of my life, I assumed books get read, authors' theories get taken up. I did not know that people could dismiss a book by looking for some minor detail and determining that they did not agree with it (hence: an error), or that the fact was a fact but had already been seen to be a fact before, a claim made without reference to the service said fact had earlier contributed to some other book (hence: ho-hum). The one serious review the book got recognized its contribution to the study of Yohanan ben Zakkai, but did not take up the larger methodological theory I had tried to define. The fault lay not with the audience but with the author. I never made explicit the methodological experiment I then proposed to carry out. I left matters inarticulate and inchoate. My guilt lay, I admit, in the assumption that things were ineffably obvious. What came to me as self-evident and beyond need for articulation I imagined would prove equally commonplace to everyone else in the world. It has taken me many years to accept the fact that the world is not made up of mind-readers, any more than, in the field in which I work, it is made up of book-readers. It is what it is. If it is to be made better, the work will have to be done one day at a time, and on one book at a time.

Yet these lessons of age, requiring me now to restate in clear and simple terms things I feared I said in an all-too-obvious way fifteen years ago, do not lead me to dismiss the project. On the contrary, Development of a Legend and the books that carried forward its basic inquiry, Rabbinic Traditions about the Pharisees before 70 and Eliezer ben Hyrcanus. The Tradition and the Man, did invoke the two modes I advocate here for explaining why sayings and stories change as they move. That is to say, I did ask systematically whether the authors of a document made changes in received sayings and stories for reasons characteristic of their document as a whole, that is the documentary theory. And I did ask systematically what we learn about the historical context and viewpoint of the authors of a document that revealed in received sayings and stories that is, the incremental-history-theory.

Let me therefore provide a reprise of how I originally exemplified these two quite distinct approaches to our problem, and then explain what I think is wrong, and remains right, with each of them.

First let me show how one might ask about the tendencies of documents' authors. Specifically will what is established overall allow us to account for shifts and changes in versions of discrete sayings and stories? For this purpose we deal with two collections of scriptural exegeses on the book of Exodus, one attributed to the school of Ishmael, the other to the school of Aqiba. I reproduce both passages, together with my discussion of them, as they originally appeared in Development of a Legend. In what follows as a comment, I.i.2 refers to Ishmael's version, I.ii.1 to Aqiba's. That is, the former derives from the Mekhilta of R. Ishmael, the latter from the Mekhilta of R. Simeon b. Yohai, who is supposed to have been a disciple of the school of Aqiba. With these facts in hand, the passages will be reasonably accessible.

2(a)   For If Thou Lift Up Thy Sword upon it (Ex. 20:25). In this connection R. Simon b. Eleazar used to say, "The altar is made to prolong the years of man and iron is made to shorten the years of man. It is not right for that which shortens life to be lifted up against that which prolongs life."

(b)   R. Yohanan b. Zakkai says, "Behold it says: Thou shalt build ... of whole stones (Deut. 27:6). They are to be stones that establish peace.

(c)   "Now, by using the method of qal vahomer, you reason: The stones for the altar do not see nor hear nor speak. Yet because they serve to establish peace between Israel and their Father in heaven, the Holy One, blessed by he, said, Thou shalt lift up no iron tool upon them (ibid., v.5). How much the more then should he who establishes peace between man and his fellow-man, between husband and wife, between city and city, between nation and nation, between family and family, between government and government, be protected so that no harm should come to him."

(Mekhilta of R. Ishmael, Bahodesh 11, ed. and trans. J. Lauterbach, II, p. 290)

On this passage I commented:

> I.ii.1, the Aqiban version given presently, substitutes sons of Torah for peacemakers
> who escape punishment; it omits the altar, and the sword shortens life becomes the
> sword as a sign of punishment. The altar does not prolong life but atones for Israel.
> I.ii.1 thus shows what the Aqiban party made of this midrash, which was none too
> palatable to them. The essential element was the exegesis on whole stones/peace.
> The function of the altar was that of making peace. Therefore peace-makers in this
> world perform the function of the altar -- and more so! This is Yohanan's essential
> idea; the functions performed by the Temple and its instruments can be replaced by
> human virtues. So the qal vehomer preserved in the Ishmaelean tradition I.1.2 and
> I.ii.5 is also originally from Yohanan, and the saying of Simeon b. Eleazar in I.i.2
> shows an early development of Yohanan's idea in its original spirit: war is bad,
> peace is good. The Aqibans therefore omitted the exegesis of peace/whole stones;
> revised the qal vehomer to make the essential virtue not peace-making but study of
> the Torah; revised Simeon's saying to make both the sword and the altar symbols of
> the attributes of the divine nature -- judgment and mercy, thus making the sword a
> good thing too; and attributed all of their revised complex to Yohanan. And they did
> an amazingly good job -- their revised version looks so much like the original that
> the careless reader would think them nearly identical. It is only when one looks
> closely that he sees the reversal of the implications.

We proceed to the version of the same saying as presented in what I then thought was the
Mekhilta to be attributed to the school of Aqiba:

> This is what Rabban Yohanan ben Zakkai says, "What was the reason iron was
> prohibited more than all [other] metals [for use in building the tabernacle (Ex.
> 20:25)]? Because the sword is made from it, and the sword is a sign of punishment,
> but the altar is a sign of atonement. A sign [means] of atonement.

> "And is this not a matter of qal vehomer? Stones, which neither see nor hear nor
> speak -- because they bring atonement between Israel and their father in heaven,
> the Holy One blessed be he said [concerning them] Thous shalt lift upon them no iron
> tool (Deut. 27:5). Sons of Torah, who are an atonement for the world, how much the
> more so that none of all the harmful forces in the world should ever touch them!"

> (Mekhilta of R. Simeon b. Yohai, Yitro 20:22, ed. Epstein-Melamed pp.
> 157-8, 1.29-31, 1-4)

On this passage I said:

> We have two separate sayings. The first is Yohanan's, that metal is prohibited
> because the sword is made of metal and is a sign of punishment, while the altar is a

sign of atonement. The second saying is the qal vehomer, that as stones should not be injured because they bring atonement, so sons of Torah should all the more so be fee of injury from harmful forces. The qal vehomer has nothing to do with Yohanan's observation, and need not be directly attributed to him, though it occurs in all formulations of this passage. It seems to be a later development.

By way of amplifying the same matter, let me give a further instance of invoking what I then imagined was a trait of Aqiban tradents to explain diverse versions of similarly connected materials:

Rabban Yohanan ben Zakkai says, "Behold it says, [With] whole stones [avanim shelemot] will you build the altar of the Lord your God (Deut. 27:5) -- Stones which make peace [shalom], and behold it is a matter of qal vehomer: Stones which do not see and do not hear and do not speak, because they bring peace between Israel and their father in heaven, Scripture says You shall not lift up iron over them (Deut. 27:6). A man who brings peace between a man and his wife, between one family and another, between one city and another, between one province and another, between one nation and another -- how much the more so that punishment should not come near him!"

I then commented:

The exegesis is practically identical with I.ii.1. The Scriptures are different. There it is "why is iron prohibited" and here it concerns the play on words: "whole stones -- stones which make peace." Atonement becomes peace, sons of Torah become peacemakers. The structure is otherwise the same; the thought is the same ("Peacemakers or those who atone for the world should come to not harm"). The details are somewhat different. Yet the differences are not very considerable. I suspect that Yohanan would have said something about the altar/altar-stones in the form of a qal vehomer. The context was Deut. 27:5 and 27:6. The play on words concerning the "whole stones" was dropped in I.ii.1, the stress on "iron" of all metals was omitted here. Strikingly, the Ishmaelean version, I.i.2, follows I.ii.5; both versions elide the whole stones play on words and the qal vehomer involving an iron tool. I should thus suppose that I.i.2 = I.ii.5. I.ii.1 differs, as I said, in omitting "whole stones" and stressing "iron." Both schools preserved an account exhibiting formal parallels (I.i.2 + I.ii.5), but the Aqibans alone preserved the other (I.ii.1), probably because they invented it. Some anterior version was available to both schools, and that anterior version derived from circles close to Yohanan himself. In a period of less than a few decades between Yohanan's death and the formation of the schools of Ishmael and Aqiba, a group of Yohanan's disciples must have put into final form materials which were subsequently made use of by both schools. This supposition is likely to be valid if the following conditions are also valid: (1) if both documents actually come from the schools to which they are attributed; (2) if the present form was edited ca. 200, if not somewhat earlier; and most important (3) if they were not expanded since that time. Then the story stands in both by A.D. 200 and was known to teachers in both schools. The common source of the story would have come substantially earlier than the founding of the two schools, ca. 100-120. In that case, as I said, the story is certainly part of the corpus of Yohanan-sayings edited by the time of Yavneh. We may safely go a step further and designate as Yavnean, all materials occurring in substantially similar form in materials ascribed to the two schools; as Ishmaelean, materials unique to that school, hence not necessarily later that Yavneh but probably from a circle at Yavneh not known or acceptable to the Aqibans; as Aqiban, materials unique to that school, within the same limitation. It would be tempting to suppose that materials unique to one or the other school were later than materials common to both, but the obvious imponderables prevent it. It is consequential, since we have no documents edited at Yavneh, to recognize that within documents edited later on are materials which probably did come from Yavneh. But it is equally noteworthy that even the materials in the earliest collections have already undergone substantial develop- ment. Primitive logia, in which stories or sayings about Yohanan are transcribed close to when they happened or were actually stated, are unavailable. In general, the closest we can come to the man himself is through secondary materials based on Yavnean traditions.

In conclusion I stated these results:

The condemnation of war and reproaches in its aftermath may likewise have been acceptable in the school whose master did not encourage the holy war of Bar Kokhba, but in any event ought to have been quite obnoxious to the one whose master did. Service of the Lord in love would have preserved the prosperity of the people, and the implied condemnation of war is present in the Ishmaelean stories about the Israelite girl.

In all I think it has been proven that no tendenz concerning Yohanan himself characterized either school. Both preserved favorable, and more important, authoritative sayings and precedents. His legal role is, if anything, slightly greater among the Aqibans than among the Ishmaeleans, but the data are too sparse for the to matter much. Most important: where the two schools differ in the sorts of stories they preserve about Yohanan, the reason for the difference is certainly found in the interests of the schools themselves, and not in their attitudes to Yohanan.

As I look back on the exercise at hand, I take comfort that, despite the obvious funda- mentalism throughout, I did have the presence of mind to specify the premises. Ac- cordingly, I emphasize that, even then, I stated as a condition that both documents had

to come from the schools to which they were attributed and represent matters in a final
way as they emerged from those schools at that time. Of course, those conditions were
not met and cannot be shown ever to have been met. So the whole in retrospect stands as
what I believe to be a good example of method and a bad example of result. But at least I
did not make things up as I went along. And the concluding, underlined judgment is one by
which I should firmly stand today.

Besides paying attention to the definitive traits of a document, we ask about how
the context of documents explains, and is explained by, alterations in received versions of
sayings and stories.

To illustrate the experiment at appealing to the context of a given document for
explanation of what the authors of that document do to peripatetic sayings, I turn to my
discussion of the later Talmudic ("Amoraic") treatment of stories about Yohanan ben
Zakkai and the conclusions I drew from the topics included in the corpus of those stories
and sayings. Admittedly, what follows focuses not upon why a given story gets or loses a
detail, or why a saying is reworded. Rather, I pay attention to the selections, out of the
larger repertoire of sayings and stories, made by a given group of tradents. The method is
the same, however, and so is the premise. That is, I claim to explain not what the
authorities did not choose, for I do not know what they did not use, but only the points of
emphasis revealed by the topics they did choose to discuss. These topical choices are
signified, over all, by their interventions into the formulation of the sayings or stories at
hand. So we know that authorities of the generation at hand took an interest in an item
because of a comment in their names made on it or because of evidence that they have
dealt with some detail or other of it. Accordingly, the approach designated incremental-historical finds exemplification in what follows.

What is said here rests on claims as to the facts of the history of the fourth-century
sages described in my History of the Jews in Babylonia. IV. The Age of Shapur II (Leiden,
1968).

> The Yohanan of Pumbedita was, therefore, primarily a political figure, a judge and
> administrator, rather than a mystic, moralist, or legislator. What interested the
> Pumbeditans was, specifically, Yohanan's relationships with the Hillelite house and
> the priesthood, his discipleship at Hillel's school, his subsequent position of equality
> with Gamaliel I and dominance over Gamaliel II. If we did not know that the
> Pumbeditans were involved in a bitter struggle with the Davidic scion of Babylonia,
> the exilarch, we might have supposed some such difficulty lay at the root of the
> Pumbeditan's interest in Yohanan. But, in fact, what is known about Pumbedita is
> precisely this: its half-century effort to raise its own funds and to preserve its
> independence from the exilarchate. The stories and references to Yohanan conform
> to that effort and serve its cause. Simply translating Gamaliel, Hillel, and the like
> to the Davidic exilarch, we find that the rabbi, or collegium of rabbis, is here
> alleged in times past to have been superior to the exilarch; to have even been
> selected disciple of the Davidide to the exclusion of the exilarch; to have proved

equal to the high priests of old; to have judged at the best court of the day; to be worthy precedent in murder trials (and the only known murder trial of Babylonian Jewish history came toward the end of this period). The prince-exilarch is to be praised if he confesses his unwitting sin and brings a sin-offering, and happy the generation whose prince does so (-- would that ours did!). Torah and good deeds avert the curse of the house of Eli -- that and not the blessing of the priest or king-messiah. The rabbi, not the exilarch, decrees what is to be done about troublesome priests. In other words, Yohanan-sayings and stories served the Pumbeditans as important precedents in their struggle with the exilarch, for it is clear that his relationships to Hillel and the Hillelites provided a vital example of what ought even now to be the case in Babylonia. It seems to me that the disproportionate interest in Yohanan at Pumbedita had no equivalent provocation in Palestine, or, if it did, the issues were argued in a different way. In any event, it is a fact that Pumbedita bears by far the largest -- practically sole -- responsibility for the Yohanan-references in the Babylonian Talmud, and Pumbeditans may even have formed some of the beraitot as we now have them. So far as I can tell, no similar interest in Yohanan was localized at any other Babylonian or Palestinian academy.

The results just now represented mark the age in which they were composed, just as much as I claim the same for the sources under discussion. The focus of interest -- the historical Yohanan ben Zakkai -- to begin with limited matters. More important, the things taken for granted as facts comprise a long and disheartening list. But even then I asked what if the Mekhilta of Ishmael does not in fact represent the historical Ishmael and his disciples? What if Simeon did not really study with Aqiba, and what if the Mekhilta of Simeon is not "Aqiban"? what if both Mekhiltas are made up in medieval times? Then every word I wrote is not wrong but beside the point.

And, of course, I now grasp the obvious fact that the entire exercise at hand in its original formulation rested on premises that I can now call mere fundamentalism. How so? At every point I took for granted that whatever is imputed to a sage really was said about him, with only one exception: Yohanan ben Zakkai. I further assumed that whatever story was told really represented the state of affairs in the time and place to which the story referred, except for the historical setting of Yohanan ben Zakkai himself. On those bases the study at hand rested. But the premises scarcely escape the simple criticism that, at each point, they share those traits of gullibility and credulity that then, as now, I have attempted to overcome. Asking how we know what Yohanan ben Zakkai really said and did, I failed to inquire into how we know that anything imputed to anyone claiming to know what Yohanan ben Zakkai really said and did also demands answers to exactly the same question. It took me a long time -- several more books -- to understand that fact and also to confront it and draw the consequences dictated by it. Others assuredly recognized the same problem. But I was the only one to try to solve it. And by redefining the foci of inquiry, I did solve it.

The reason that <u>Development of a Legend</u> made so little impression in its day, however, is not because it was insufficiently critical. By the standards not only of that day but also of the present age, a decade and a half and many books later, <u>Development</u> remains too radical in its methods, in its points of fundamental insistence, for the generality of scholars in the field to confront. If they respond to the book at all, it is by pointing out misprints. This means they cannot take up the challenge of the book and all that followed it. Why the avoidance? Because if <u>Development of a Legend</u> points to what work must be done, then the sort of scholarly work people want to do cannot be done. It is one thing to recognize the utter obsolescence of everything accomplished in the critical study of the history of the Jews and of Judaism in late antiquity, so far as the rabbinic canon constitutes the principal literary source. It is quite another to insist, as I did and do insist, that everything people now propose as a scholarly program rests on the same false premises.

The way lies open to inquiry into the relationship of text to context, of detail to main point of insistence. Results of the inquiry will tell us something about why a given set of ideas became self-evident and remained manifestly "right" for a very long time. Then we also may find a clue on why those same ideas, that same system of a world-view and a way of life characteristic of a single social group for a long span of history, lost the trait of self-evidence and became manifestly irrelevant. That is to say, at stake is how to interpret the history of Judaism: its formation and persistence, change and renewal. The first task is to describe, analyze, and interpret the facts in hand. Among these facts, the obvious ones concern how, to the naked eye, a story will change as it is told and retold, a saying will undergo revision when it is repeated.

Let me close by placing into the correct, appropriately large, context the humble facts that have occupied us for so long. Why, specifically, do I regard as indicative the persistence and transformation of sayings and stories? And what do I hope will be indicated? The answer lies in the three basic dimensions by which we take the measure of every document of the canon of Judaism, from the Mishnah through the Bavli. (I elaborate on this matter in the appendix that follows.)

Every book of the canon stands by itself. Each is <u>autonomous</u>.

Except for the Mishnah and Scripture, every book in the canon refers back to some other book. Some of the books relate as a whole to the Mishnah. They serve as exegeses and amplifications of the Mishnah. Other s depend upon Scripture. So every book in the canon, except for the Mishnah and Scripture, is not only autonomous but also <u>connected</u> to some other book. The autonomy is limited by connection.

And, finally, all of the books together, Scripture and the Mishnah, Tosefta and the Talmuds, Sifra, the two Sifres, Genesis Rabbah, Leviticus Rabbah, and the rest of the compositions, viewed whole, all at once, and in their entirety, constitute the "one whole Torah of Moses, our rabbi." That continuity is not merely the <u>post facto</u> assertion of the believing community. It also constitutes a fact to be induced from evidence by detailed inquiry into the shared conceptions and values, alleged at the end of the process of the formation of the canon as a whole, to characterize all documents of the canon. Looking backward, I should not be prepared to make an exception, in that characterization, even of Scriptures. That is so even though sages, in the manner of their age and all ages before and since, read into Scripture whatever they wished to see there. That qualification should not present an exception to this simple claim: the documents all together do constitute a canon. So they establish a <u>continuity</u> from one to the next and among them all.

Two of the three dimensions of the canon -- autonomy, connection, continuity -- obviously appear to the naked eye: autonomy and connection. How so? A document, by definition, stands alone and autonomous. The Tosefta, the Mishnah, the two Sifres each will afford examination on its own. The connection of all of the compositions of the canon to either Scripture or the Mishnah comes to vivid expression in the fundamental redactional preferences of each document. The Tosefta is organized in accord with the order of passages of the Mishnah, the two Talmuds with the same structure, and all compilations of scriptural exegeses ("midrashim") follow the order of verses in the book of Scripture they allegedly explain. The variations in degree of explicit dependence, for redactional order and structure, on one or the other of the two base-documents make little difference.

But when we ask whether and how the documents form a continuity from one to the next and, among all of them together constitute a canon, where shall we look for relevant data? I see only two sources of facts for the assessment of where and how documents relate as a whole to one another, not only back to a single shared source of structure supplied by Scripture or the Mishnah. One source flows from shared conceptions, symbols, fundamental and everywhere-definitive values. The other source derives from shared sayings and stories. The contrast speaks for itself.

The former source -- shared symbols -- flows at random and aimlessly, much as at floodtide the sea overcomes the shore, and the river its banks. We never know the limits. We form impressions of where the boundaries lie, only to discover, as water recedes and advances, that, short of going out and wading around, we have missed the mark dividing dry shore from ocean or river. But if we wade out in the shifting tide, we may drown. So too if we aimlessly seize upon one ubiquitous value or another and allege that one congeries defines what is shared, uniform, continuous, and another does not, we shall drown in facts. We shall never have a clear criterion for knowing when we are right, and when we are wrong. Once need not dismiss as impressionistic the great and valiant efforts of such exemplary scholars as George Foot Moore and Max Kadushin to recognize the failures they left behind. The field of learning in the nineteenth and twentieth century is strewn with the carcasses of abandoned definitions of "Judaism," including the system of Judaism revealed by the canon concluded in late antiquity.

But there endures that other source of information -- shared sayings and stories -- on what moves in continuity from one document to another. What <u>in fact</u> travels from the Mishnah to the Tosefta to the Yerushalmi to the Bavli, or from a Mekhilta to the Tosefta, to the Fathers according to Rabbi Nathan, or hither and yon or here and there? The peripatetic saying and the thrice-told tale constitute concrete, material proofs of the actualities. They define facts of continuity that to begin with make possible the claim that autonomous documents relate not in general but very particularly. Then we may see, in the character of detail, that main point that we seek. The shape of the whole, the measure of the dimension of continuity -- these to begin with emerge from the simple fact that the same saying or story will be shared among two or more documents of the canon. That validates the claim of continuity, though obviously not exhausting what is meant by the claim. But, in the details of what is like and what is unlike in the traveling tale and the peripatetic saying we see clearly, without distortion, what is common to important components of the canon of Judaism. True, all we have at the moment is detail. But of canonical Judaism we cannot speak just now, except to say that, after all, God really does live in the details.

APPENDIX

AUTONOMY, CONNECTION, CONTINUITY:
THE THREE DIMENSIONS OF A TEXT OF FORMATIVE JUDAISM

[Plenary presentation, "How My Mind Has Changed," Society of Biblical
Literature, Chicago, December 10, 1984.]

When we take up a book that speaks of a single document in the canon of Judaism
and propose to describe, analyze, and interpret that book in particular, we violate the
lines of order and system that have characterized earlier studies of these same
documents. Until now, people have tended to treat all of the canonical texts as
testimonies to a single system and structure, that is, to Judaism. What sort of testimonies texts provide varies according to the interest of the scholars, students, and saints
who study them. Scholars look for meanings of words and phrases, better versions of a
text. For them all canonical documents equally serve as a treasury of philological facts
and variant readings. Students also look for the sense of words and phrases and follow a
given phrase hither and yon, as their teachers direct them on their treasure hunt. Saints
study all texts equally, looking for God's will and finding testimonies to God in each
component of the Torah of Moses our Rabbi.

Among none of these circles will the discrete description, analysis, and interpretation of a single text make sense. Why not? Because all texts ordinarily are taken to
form a common statement, "Torah" in the mythic setting, "Judaism" in the theological
one. Since I spent the first half of my scholarly life trying to use all of the texts in the
canon, more or less without differentiation and equally, to answer historical questions, I
participated in the approach now rejected. I thought that what was definitive, what laid
forth lines of structure and order, was not the text at hand but the problem I had defined.
So I did not tease out of the texts the threads of context, looking for the fabric's
coherence in its small details, in the interstices of warp and woof. I set up my own loom.
I pulled the texts apart and made them into mere threads, then rewove them my way. On
that, as is clear, I have changed my mind, and, I would claim, my field.

Let me spell out the change at hand and then briefly address Judaism: The Evidence
of the Mishnah and Judaism in Society: The Evidence of the Yerushalmi, the principal
documents of the day. To begin with, however, I emphasize that nothing I say will
surprise scholars in the biblical fields of Old and New Testament, Israel in ancient times
and earliest Christianity. They understand that the work of the hour does not demand
more harmonies of the Gospels. They rigorously debate issues of orthodoxy and hetero-
doxy in earliest Christianity and whether and where, among the diverse Christianities,
they may find patterns of Christian truth. In the nineteenth century they abandoned any
notion of using all of the (canonical) texts equally and for a single purpose. In the

twentieth, such giants as H.E.W. Turner and Walter Bauer ended for all time the simple notions that you can open a book, thumb the pages and pull out a Christianity. When my mind changed, under the influence of the examples of my colleagues in other areas of history, the history and comparison of religion, and, obviously, in the biblical areas and those of earliest Christianity, I had to relive two hundred years of scholarship in twenty years. Permit me, then, to report in my field what are methodological commonplaces of other fields.

We begin with theology and move to texts. For the hermeneutical issue defines the result of description, analysis, and interpretation. From today's perspective the entire canon of Judaism -- "the one whole Torah of Moses, our rabbi" -- equally and at every point testifies to the entirety of Judaism. Why so? Because all documents in the end form components of a single system. Each makes its contribution to the whole. If, therefore, we wish to know what "Judaism" or, more accurately, "the Torah," teaches on any subject, we are able to draw freely on sayings relevant to that subject wherever they occur in the entire canon of Judaism. Guided only by the taste and judgment of the great sages of the Torah, as they have addressed the question at hand, we thereby describe "Judaism."

Composites of sayings drawn from diverse books in no way violate the frontiers and boundaries that distinguish one part of the canon from some other part of the same canon. Why not? It is a theological conviction that defines the hermeneutic. Viewed as serving the Torah, which is a single and continuous revelation, all frontiers, all boundaries stand only at the outer limits of the whole. Within, as the saying has it, "There is neither earlier nor later," that is to say, temporal considerations do not apply. But if temporal distinctions make no difference, no others do either.

Accordingly, as Judaism comes to informed expression in the Judaic pulpit, in the Judaic classroom, above all in the lives and hearts and minds of Jews loyal to Judaism, all parts of the canon of Judaism speak equally authoritatively. All parts, all together, present us with one harmonious world-view and homogenous way of life, one Torah ("Judaism") for all Israel. That view of "the Torah," that is to say, of the canon of Judaism, characterizes every organized movement within Judaism as we now know it, whether Reform or Orthodox, whether Reconstructionist or Conservative, whether in the "Exile" (diaspora) or in the State of Israel. How so? Among circles of Judaism indifferent to considerations of time and place, anachronism and context, every document, whenever brought to closure, testifies equally to that single system. For those circles Judaism emerges at a single moment ("Sinai"), but comes to expression in diverse times and places, so that any composition that falls into the category of Torah serves, without further differentiation, to tell us about the substance of Judaism, its theology and law.

An important qualification, however, has now to make its mark. Among those circles of Judaism to whom historical facts do make a difference, for example, Orthodoxy in the West, Reconstructionist, Conservative and Reform Judaism and the like, considerations of what was completed earlier as against what came to closure only later on, for instance, in the second century as against the eighteenth century, do make some difference. Earlier documents provide more compelling and authoritative evidence than later ones. But even in the view of this other sector of Judaism, all documents, if not everywhere equally authoritative, still form part of a continuous whole, Judaism. The distinction between the two positions makes no material difference. Why not? Because both circles hold as self-evident that the numerous components of the canon of Judaism form a continuity, beginning, middle, and end. That is why considerations of priority and of closure, should these considerations find their way into discourse at all, change little and affect nothing. Torah is Torah, early, middle, and late. And so it is -- except from the perspective of one outside the magic circle of the faith. Here we ask exactly how various documents became "Torah," what each document added to the whole, in which ways do the several documents relate to one another and to the larger system, and so, in all, reverting to mythic language, what makes Torah Torah.

For a person engaged in such an inquiry into the formation of Judaism studied through the analysis of the literary evidence of the canon, documents stand in three relationships to one another and to the system of which they form part, that is, to Judaism, as a whole. The specification of these relationships constitutes the principal premise of my work. It is a premise since, to begin with, the relationships I perceive derive not inductively, from the documents at hand, but from the mind of the one who turns to analyze the documents. So at this point I cannot claim to approach matters inductively.

Each document, as a matter of theory, is to be seen all by itself, that is, as autonomous of all others.

Each document, again as a matter of theory, is to be examined for its relationships with other documents universally regarded as falling into the same classification, as Torah. So each text is connected to others.

And, finally, each document is to be allowed to take its place as part of the undifferentiated aggregation of documents that, all together, constitute the canon of Judaism, that is to say, "Torah." So each text stands in continuity with others.

Simple logic makes self-evident the proposition that, if a document comes down to us within its own framework, as a complete book with a beginning, middle, and end, in preserving that book, the canon presents us with a document on its own and not solely as part of a larger composition or construct. So we too see the document as it reaches us, that is, as autonomous.

If, second, a document contains materials shared verbatim or in substantial content with other documents of its classification, or if one document refers to the contents of other documents, then the several documents that clearly wish to engage in conversation with one another have to address one another. That is to say, we have to seek for the marks of connectedness, asking for the meaning of those connections.

Finally, since, as I said at the outset, the community of the faithful of Judaism, in all of the contemporary expressions of Judaism, concur that documents held to be authoritative constitute one whole, seamless "Torah," that is, a complete and exhaustive statement of God's will for Israel and humanity, we take as our further task the description of the whole out of the undifferentiated testimony of all of its parts. These components in the theological context are viewed, as is clear, as equally authoritative for the composition of the whole: one, continuous system. In taking up such a question, we address a problem not of theology alone, though it is a correct theological conviction, but one of description, analysis, and interpretation of an entirely historical order.

In this way we may hope to trace the literary evidence -- which is the only evidence we have -- for the formation of Judaism, what it is, how it works. By seeing the several components of the canon of Judaism in sequence, first, one by one, then, one after the other, and finally, all together all at once, we may trace the literary side of the history of Judaism. We may see how a document came into being on its own, in its context (so far as we may posit the character of that context). We interpret the document at its site. As a matter of fact, moreover, all documents of the rabbinic canon except for the Hebrew Scriptures relate to prior ones, on the one side, and all, especially the Scriptures, stand before those to follow, on the other. The Mishnah normally is understood to rest upon the written Torah, and, later in its history in Judaism, came to be called the oral Torah. So even the Mishnah stands not distinct and autonomous, but contingent and dependent. The two Talmuds rest upon the Mishnah, and the several compilations of exegeses of Scripture, called "midrashim", rest upon Scripture. So, in all, like the bones of the body, each book is connected to others (with Scripture and the Mishnah the backbone). All together they form a whole, a frame that transcends the parts and imparts proportion, meaning, and harmony to them.

The bones of the body develop more or less in shared stages, however, while the documents of the Torah, the canon of Judaism, developed in a sequence. The order, if not so linear as it seems on the surface, is mostly clear. First came Scripture, then the Mishnah, then the Talmud of the Land of Israel and earlier compilations of biblical exegeses, then the Talmud of Babylonia and the later compilations of biblical exegeses. In that sequence of the important texts we shall find whatever evidence of growth, development, and change, as we shall ever have available to tell us the history of Judaism. To complete the matter, what do we hope to learn as we relate growth, development, and change in the history of Judaism, traced through the formation and character of its canon, to the growth, development, and change in the history of the Jewish people? It is not only to describe and analyze, but also to explain, the history of the formation of Judaism. That is to say, we may frame theories not only on the formative history of the world-view and way of life we call Judaism, but on the reasons that the history went the route it took, rather than some other route. How so? We may ask why people thought what they thought and did what they did, rather than thinking other thoughts and doing other things. When we can relate the ideas people held and the way they lived their life to the context in which they found themselves, we shall have reached that level of interpretation at which present and past come together in the setting of shared human existence: the meeting of text and context. But we stand at a distance from that elusive goal.

What I have said in general makes sense in particular of Judaism: The Evidence of the Mishnah and Judaism in Society: The Evidence of the Yerushalmi. I mention two

other titles, Judaism and Scripture: The Evidence of Leviticus Rabbah and Judaism in
Conclusion: The Evidence of the Bavli. These four works yield yet a final one, on which I
now work, The Oral Torah: An Introduction. What each item proposes is two exercises
which are one. First, I wish to describe a single document. Second, I also want to address
to a given document one important question. My premise is that a document ordinarily is
about something. Except for anthologies of information, people write books to make
points, to answer questions, to say something important. In the ancient world people
copied and preserved books at great expense, so books had to matter. The premise, then,
that a given document tells us something important to those who wrote it and their
successors, seems to me self-evident.

It follows that we have to find out what polemic, what point of insistence, what
aspect of self-evidence a given text reveals. As I have stressed in every work of mine, we
begin the search with the smallest details, we then ask what the details of the text
repeatedly stress. This commonly emerges not from what the text says, but from how it
says what it says. In the main beams of rhetoric, in the repeated details, ubiquitous,
implicit, self-evident, and therefore definitive, I claim to find that principal message that
speaks for the work as a whole. The deepest structures of syntax may convey the
principles of order. The techniques of rhetoric, broadly construed, properly understood,
may speak also to us. They accordingly may deliver a text's substantive message through
the forms of proportion and of intelligible, therefore logical, speech.

About what main point do the texts at hand then speak? I see the Mishnah as a
complete statement of an entire system. I see the documents of succession, typified by
the Yerushalmi, as large-scale efforts to translate the Mishnah's philosophical system into
social order. I see counterpart documents of Scripture-exegesis, which treat Scripture as
the two Talmuds treat the Mishnah, as exercises in the construction of dialogue between
Scripture and the Mishnah. And I see the final document of the canon, the Bavli, as a
synthetic work of restatement and completion. The Bavli joins the two main lines of
order and systemic structure, the Mishnah and Scripture, and makes them the basis for its
proportions and the foundations of its social order.

In my view the various documents of the canon of Judaism produced in late antiquity
demand a different hermeneutic altogether from the one of homogenization and
harmonization, the ahistorical and anti-contextual one I have outlined. It is one that does
not harmonize but that differentiates. It is a hermeneutic shaped to teach us how to read
the texts at hand one by one and in a particular context, exactly in the way in which we
read any other text bearing cultural and social insight. The texts stand not as self-evi-
dently important but only as examples, sources of insight for a quite neutral inquiry. Let
me spell out what I think is at issue between the established hermeneutic and the one I
propose.

The three key-words of the inherited hermeneutic are continuity, uniqueness, and
survival. Scholars who view the texts as continuous with one another seek what is unique
in the system formed by the texts as a whole. With the answer to what is unique, they
propose to explain the survival of Israel, the Jewish people. Hence: continuity, uniqueness, survival.

The words to encapsulate the hermeneutic I espouse are these: <u>description</u>, <u>analysis</u>, and <u>interpretation</u>. I am trying to learn how to <u>describe</u> the constituents of the canon, viewed individually, each in its distinctive context. I wish to discover appropriate <u>analytical</u> tools, questions to lead me from description of one text to comparison and contrast between two or more texts of the canon. Only at the end do I address the question of <u>interpretation</u>: how do all of the texts of the canon at hand flow together into a single continuous statement, a "Judaism."

Within the inherited hermeneutic of continuity, survival, and uniqueness, the existence of the group defines the principal concern, an inner-facing one, hence the emphasis on uniqueness in quest, in continuities, for the explanation of survival. Within the proposed hermeneutic of description, analysis, and interpretation, by contrast, the continued survival of a "unique" group does not frame the issue. For my purposes, it is taken for granted, for the group is not the main thing at all. The problematic emerges from without. What I want to know is not how and why the group survived so as to help it survive some more. It is how to describe the society and culture contained within, taken as a given, how to interpret an enduring world-view and way of life, expressed by the artifacts in hand. How did, and does, the group work?

So I claimed that the results of the literary inquiry will prove illuminating for the study of society and culture. I have now to explain why I think so. The answer lies in our will and capacity to generalize, out of details, a judgment on a broad issue of culture, as it is exemplified in the small problem at hand. The issue here is secular. True, I too ask how the components of the canon as a whole form a continuity. I wonder why this document in particular survived to speak for the whole. But for me the answers to these questions generate theories, promise insight for the study of other canonical religions. So far as I shall succeed, it will be because I can learn from these other canonical religions. I have tried to learn from, and also to teach something to, those who study the history, the thought, the social reality, of religions that, like Judaism, form enduring monuments to the power of humanity to endure and to prevail so far.

ARN
  152, 157, 158, 163
ARNa
  17, 19-21
ARNa
  146-48, 151-53, 157, 158
ARNb
  151-53
Abbaye
  25, 28, 93
Abot
  17, 33
Abraham
  13, 14, 16, 79
Abtalion (Avtalion)
  79-83, 104, 108, 110, 160, 161, 164,
  165, 167-69
Alexander Jannaeus
  26, 28
Alexander of Macedonia
  26, 28, 37-39
Amoraic
  63, 67, 70, 72, 89, 93, 94, 116, 163,
  186
Antiochus Epiphanes
  27
Aqiba
  14-16, 22, 82, 83, 136, 137, 154, 155,
  182-84, 187
Aramaic
  25, 26, 28, 29, 40, 41, 53, 90, 110,
  111, 165
Avot
  33, 66, 163, 165-68
Babylonia
  1, 41, 51, 89, 90, 94, 98, 104, 128,
  140, 147, 186, 187, 194
Babylonian
  7, 15, 16, 19-25, 35, 36, 39-41, 46, 47,
  50, 51, 61, 66, 67, 70, 72, 77, 88-90,
  93, 94, 97, 104, 107, 110, 113, 116,
  119, 121, 122, 127, 132, 138, 139,
  141, 142, 147, 152, 153, 157, 162,
  168, 187
Babylonian Talmud
  7, 22, 36, 40, 51, 70, 110, 132, 152,
  187
Bar Kokhba
  22, 185
Bauer, Walter
  191
Bavli
  1, 2, 5, 7, 8, 10-12, 17, 20-23, 25, 29,
  159, 180, 188, 189, 195
Ben Sira
  77, 166

Bible
  8
Biography
  1, 7
Boethusians
  55, 61
Chronicles
  8, 174
Deuteronomy
  8, 21
Development of a Legend
  1, 11, 181, 182, 188
Eleazar
  9, 12-17, 26-28, 52, 116, 144, 148,
  173, 174, 182, 183
Eleazar b. Arakh
  12, 173, 174
Eleazar b. Azariah
  9
Eliezer
  1, 18-22, 52, 53, 67, 115, 116, 151,
  152, 154, 155, 157, 182
Elijah
  70-72
Exodus
  8, 182
Ezekiel
  9, 12, 174
Feldman, L.H.
  27
Gaius Caligula
  41
Gamaliel
  21, 22, 125-27, 129, 131, 132, 155,
  157, 163-69, 186
Genesis
  8, 137, 188
Gibbon
  29
God
  13, 18, 19, 27, 39, 93, 112, 120, 138,
  142, 145, 146, 148, 184, 190, 191, 193
Gospels
  8, 191
Green, William Scott
  4, 173-75
Halperin, David J.
  172-75, 180, 181
Hananiah
  14, 15, 21, 22
Hebrew
  8, 25, 40, 41, 46, 111, 194
Hezekiah
  18

Hillel
  22, 23, 51, 65, 80-82, 93, 97-104,
  108-110, 111-23, 135-37, 160-69, 186,
  187
Hiyya
  8, 104
Honi
  70
Hyrcanus, John
  1, 27, 28, 116, 151, 182
Israeli
  2, 3, 9, 151
Jacob b. Idi
  17, 19-21
Jastrow
  93
Jerusalem
  12, 49, 63, 80-82, 85, 87, 89, 120,
  122, 131, 146, 151, 155, 156, 162,
  164, 166, 167
Jesus
  8
Job
  126, 183
Jonathan b. Uzziel
  23, 24, 96
Josephus
  25, 27-29
Joshua
  14-17, 19-22, 26, 55, 115, 116,
  135-37, 152, 154, 155, 157, 160-65,
  167-69
Joshua b. Levi
  17, 20, 115, 116
Joshua b. Perahiah
  26, 55, 160, 161, 163-65, 167-69
Judah
  8, 14, 18, 21-23, 26, 28, 49-51, 55-57,
  59, 61-66, 82, 87, 89, 125, 131, 132,
  160-64, 167-69
Judah b. Tabbai
  26, 51, 55, 56, 59, 62-64, 66, 160-62,
  164, 167
Judah the Patriarch
  8, 82, 132, 162, 168
Judaism
  1-3, 7-9, 179, 188-96
Kings
  8, 18, 19
Lieberman, S.
  3, 34, 127, 161
Meir
  47, 62, 63, 131, 132, 161-63, 168
Mekhilta
  10-12, 15, 16, 57, 62, 79, 97, 141-44,
  147, 148, 182, 183, 187, 189
Menahem
  93, 94, 160-62, 167
Merkavah
  12, 16, 172, 173, 175, 181
Midrash
  100, 102, 183

Midrashim
  7, 152, 189, 194
Mishnah
  1, 7, 8, 17, 22, 23, 37, 38, 50, 53, 70,
  72, 81-83, 94, 100, 103, 118, 125, 132,
  152, 159, 167, 171, 172, 174, 188,
  189, 191, 194, 195
Moses
  49, 113, 136-40, 164, 166-68, 188,
  191, 192
Nasi
  62, 63, 69, 82, 106, 108, 109, 161-63,
  168
Nazirite
  36
Nazirites
  35, 36, 72, 73, 77
Nittai the Arbelite
  55, 160, 163, 164, 167-69
Numbers
  8
Palestine
  99, 187
Palestinian
  15-17, 19-25, 36, 41, 46, 47, 50, 51,
  61, 63, 66, 70, 72, 77, 88-90, 93, 94,
  97, 99, 104, 110, 113, 116, 119, 129,
  133, 139, 142, 146, 147, 152, 162,
  169, 187
Pharisee
  28
Pharisees
  1, 11, 26-28, 31, 166, 182
Proverbs
  77
Sadducee
  90, 131
Sadducees
  28, 55, 59, 61
Samuel
  8, 23, 49, 50, 87, 89, 115, 116, 137
Scripture
  1, 7, 11, 22, 33, 35, 36, 71, 75, 97, 98,
  139-43, 147, 184, 188, 189, 194, 195
Scriptures
  8, 111, 146, 184, 189, 194
Shammai
  23-25, 51, 65, 80-82, 93, 95, 96,
  117-23, 160-69
Shemaiah
  79-83, 104, 108, 110, 160-62, 164,
  167-69
Sifra
  3, 7, 52, 53, 66, 67, 98-100, 131, 140,
  143, 144, 188
Sifre
  21, 22, 34-37, 67, 70, 82, 94, 95, 100,
  102, 135-38, 144, 147, 148
Simeon
  12, 14, 16, 26-28, 33-47, 51, 55-57,
  59, 61-74, 77, 79, 90, 97, 131-33,
  160-69, 182, 183, 187

Simeon b. Gamaliel
131, 163-69
Simeon b. Shetah
26-28, 51, 55, 59, 62, 63, 65, 66, 69,
160-62, 164, 167, 169
Simeon the Just
33, 34, 36-42, 164, 166, 167
Talmud
1, 3, 7, 10, 11, 21, 22, 28, 36, 40, 41,
46, 51, 70, 77, 110, 132, 146, 147,
152, 169, 187, 194
Talmudic historians
3, 9, 11
Targum
126, 127
Torah
26, 33, 49, 50, 55, 56, 60, 75, 76, 99,
101-104, 119, 143, 144, 153, 164-66,
168, 171, 172, 183, 184, 187, 188,
191-95
Tosefta
3, 7, 8, 10-12, 15, 16, 25, 34-36, 40,
41, 47, 57, 81, 82, 90, 95, 104, 110,
118, 119, 136, 147, 152, 173, 174,
188, 189
Turner, H.E.W.
191

Ulla
37
Yavneh
21, 22, 115, 116, 152, 153, 155, 157,
158, 163, 185
Yerushalmi
1-3, 7, 8, 10-12, 17, 22, 23, 189, 191,
194, 195
Yohanan
1, 9, 11-23, 25, 28, 37, 41, 49, 50, 64,
85-87, 89, 90, 125-27, 129, 135-48,
151-58, 160, 162-64, 166-69, 171,
172, 174, 181-87
Yohanan b. Zakkai
9, 163, 166, 168, 169, 172, 174, 182
Yohanan the High Priest
25, 37, 41, 85, 89
Yose
14, 16, 17, 21, 23, 24, 49-53, 64, 118,
119, 125-27, 160-64, 166-69
Yose b. Yoezer
49, 52, 64, 160-62, 164, 167-69
Yose b. Yohanan
49, 50, 64, 160, 162, 164, 167-69
Zealots
158

BROWN JUDAIC STUDIES SERIES

Continued from back cover

140040	Israeli Childhood Stories of the Sixties: Yizhar, Aloni, Shahar, Kahana-Carmon	Gideon Telpaz
140041	Formative Judaism II: Religious, Historical, and Literary Studies	Jacob Neusner
140042	Judaism in the American Humanities II: Jewish Learning and the New Humanities	Jacob Neusner
140043	Support for the Poor in the Mishnaic Law of Agriculture: Tractate Peah	Roger Brooks
140044	The Sanctity of the Seventh Year: A Study of Mishnah Tractate Shebiit	Louis E. Newman
140045	Character and Context: Studies in the Fiction of Abramovitsh, Brenner, and Agnon	Jeffrey Fleck
140046	Formative Judaism III: Religious, Historical, and Literary Studies	Jacob Neusner
140047	Pharaoh's Counsellors: Job, Jethro, and Balaam in Rabbinic and Patristic Tradition	Judith Baskin
140048	The Scrolls and Christian Origins: Studies in the Jewish Background of the New Testament	Matthew Black
140049	Approaches to Modern Judaism	Marc Lee Raphael
140050	Mysterious Encounters at Mamre and Jabbok	William T. Miller
140051	The Empire and the Subject Nations: The Middle Eastern Policy of Imperial Rome	Eliezer Paltiel
140052	Sparda by the Bitter Sea: Imperial Interaction in Western Anatolia	Jack Balcer
140053	Hermann Cohen: The Challenge of a Religion of Reason	William Kluback
140054	Approaches to Judaism in Medieval Times	David R. Blumenthal
140055	In the Margins of the Yerushalmi: Glosses on the English Translation	Jacob Neusner
140056	Approaches to Modern Judaism II	Marc Lee Raphael
140057	Approaches to Judaism in Medieval Times II	David R. Blumenthal
140058	Approaches to Ancient Judaism VI	William Scott Green
140059	The Commerce of the Sacred: Mediation of the Divine Among Jews in the Graeco-Roman Diaspora	Jack N. Lightstone
140060	Major Trends in Formative Judaism I: Society and Symbol in Political Crisis	Jacob Neusner
140061	Major Trends in Formative Judaism II: Texts, Contents, and Contexts	Jacob Neusner
140062	A History of the Jews in Babylonia. I: The Parthian Period	Jacob Neusner
140063	The Talmud of Babylonia: An American Translation. XXXII: Tractate Arakhin	Jacob Neusner
140064	Ancient Judaism: Debates and Disputes	Jacob Neusner
140065	Prayers Alleged to Be Jewish: An Examination of the Constitutiones Apostolorum	David Fiensy
140066	The Legal Methodology of Hai Gaon	Tsvi Groner
140067	From Mishnah to Scripture: The Problem of the Unattributed Saying	Jacob Neusner
140068	Halakhah in a Theological Dimension: Essays on the Interpenetration of Law and Theology in Judaism	David Novak